You're Made *for a* God-Sized Dream

Books by Holley Gerth

You're Already Amazing

The "Do What You Can" Plan (ebook)

"Holley held my hand as I helped launch one of the biggest, scariest, most beautiful God-sized dreams I've ever been a part of. It impacted thousands of women from over twenty countries. This book is the blueprint that helped me make it through. I lived Holley's words throughout all the speed bumps, pitfalls, and loud voices of fear pummeling the inside of my head and the pit of my stomach. Holley's encouragement is practical, grounded in experience, and laced with grace, gospel, grit, and enough experience to convince you not to quit when the fear gets the loudest but to press on and into the God who gave you the dream in the first place. Everyone needs a guide when they're on a God-sized journey. With a sense of humor and a side of cheerleading, Holley is the one I'd recommend with two thumbs up."

—**Lisa-Jo Baker**, social media manager for DaySpring, community manager for the website (in)courage, and visionary for the (in)RL conference

"God has a dream for you. Yes, *you* have a God-sized dream, even if you don't know what it is yet. Holley will show you how to tap into your dream and thrive in it. You'll feel like you have a personal guide to help you overcome your fears, define your dream, and understand how to pursue it with confidence. Holley is the encouraging friend you'll need for the exciting adventure into your God-sized dream."

—**Stephanie S. Bryant**, cofounder of (in)courage and creative mastermind at S. Bryant Social Marketing

"I can't remember the last time I turned the pages of a book so eagerly. Holley's words have revolutionized my way of thinking with such a simple concept: that my dreams can't be bigger than God. If he's in my soul-planted dreams—and I think he is—then why wouldn't he also craft my life to fulfill those very same dreams? Holley is remarkably gifted at explaining universal heart truths to those of us in different seasons of life and then equipping each of us with the motivation to make those truths a reality. I thank God for my friend, this gifted writer Holley."

—**Tsh Oxenreider**, author of *Organized Simplicity*, blogger behind SimpleMom.net, and creative director of SimpleLivingMedia.com

"Reading this book is like having your own personal cheerleader by your side as you pursue your God-sized dream. Holley will challenge you to overcome your fear and stop sabotaging yourself, all the while reminding you that you're amazing and perfectly designed for turning your dream into reality."

—**Mary Carver**, author of the blog *Giving Up on Perfect* and monthly columnist at (in)courage

"Reading *You're Made for a God-Sized Dream* isn't like reading at all; it's more like a visit with a trusted friend, the one who speaks truth and wisdom into your life and helps you to see yourself the way God sees you. I have no idea how Holley accomplishes this (does every reader feel like they've found a new best friend?), but she does! God used this dream of Holley's to help me believe in the dreams he's seeded in *my* soul—those urgings that won't go away, the things that hide in secret places but are clawing for escape. Sifting through Holley's insights, I feel almost like I have *permission* to dream now; I didn't realize how much I swept those hopes to the corners of my heart."

—**Robin Dance**, author of the blog *Pensieve*

"Holley Gerth is a cheerleader for women with God-sized dreams of all shapes and sizes. She'll encourage and equip you to pursue the dream God planted in your heart."

—**Dawn Camp**, writer, photographer, and author of the blog *My Home Sweet Home Online*

"Holley is every woman's sister and a profound writer whose words touch the farthest corners of a woman's heart. Relational and personal, *You're Made for a God-Sized Dream* will show you how to give wings to your dreams as you fly straight to the heart of God."

—**Kristen Strong**, writer and author of the blog *Chasing Blue Skies*

"I used to think God-sized dreams were only for people with perfect faith, powerhouse social media platforms, or personalities that thrive in a high-stakes environment. Then I met Holley Gerth, and little by little she helped me realize that God-sized dreams are for everyone, including me. Including you. Combining her rock-solid wisdom as a certified life coach with her sincerely encouraging heart, Holley invites you to take a peek at the God-sized dreams designed specifically for you."

—**Deidra Riggs**, owner and writer of *Jumping Tandem*, managing editor for TheHighCalling.org, and contributing writer for (in)courage

You're Made *for a* God-Sized Dream

Opening the Door to All God Has for You

Holley Gerth

Revell
a division of Baker Publishing Group
Grand Rapids, Michigan

Published by Revell
a division of Baker Publishing Group
P.O. Box 6287, Grand Rapids, MI 49516-6287
www.revellbooks.com

Printed in the United States of America

Library of Congress Cataloging-in-Publication Data is on file at the Library of Congress in Washington, DC.

ISBN 978-0-8007-2061-2

13 14 15 16 17 18 7 6 5 4 3 2 1

For the

God-sized dreamers ~

you know who you are

Contents

1

The **"More"** You're Made For

She whispers it into the phone, almost too softly for me to hear.

"I just . . . have this desire in my heart that won't go away."

She lists off reasons why it won't work, why this isn't the right time, and how she feels odd for even thinking about it in the first place.

When she pauses for a deep, unsure breath, I slip in these words: "It sounds like you have a God-sized dream."

"A what?" she responds with a bit of wonder in her voice.

I smile and share more about desire and hope, what it means to make it to your personal Promised Land, and how everything is going to be different now.

I understand God-sized dreams because I've lived them. And once you have a taste, there's no going back to life as you knew it before.

You may say, "But I don't have big dreams."

Exactly.

The size of the dream isn't what matters.

I believe everyone has God-sized dreams. It's not about how big or small they are, because he creates each one to perfectly fit the size of *your* heart.

Your dream might be to move across the world and start a nonprofit organization that cares for orphans—what looks like a grand adventure in the world's eyes.

Or your dream might be to stay right in your small town and raise your kids so that they grow into strong men and women—what looks like something fairly ordinary in the world's eyes.

Both matter equally.

And both are God-sized dreams.

It's not about what you do as much as *how* you do it. It's about pursuing life with passion and purpose and going with God wherever he leads.

It's about not settling. It's about tenaciously believing *you're made for more.*

Not as in "bigger house, fancier car, more luxurious lifestyle."

No, my friend, I mean "more of Jesus, more of what he's created you to be, more of what he's called you to do." Less of you, actually, and more of all he is and all he has for you—which is beyond what you can even imagine.

I'm thinking of you right now, wherever you are—perhaps holding this book in your hand in the aisle of a bookstore, curled up on your couch, or on a long flight—and I wish I could be right beside you. I'd like to pour you a cup of coffee or tea and listen long and hard to the things you're afraid to tell anyone: the hopes that feel silly, the dreams that seem like dares, the quiet longings of your heart that get especially loud sometimes.

I'd nod, look you in the eyes, and say, "Don't let that go. Don't hide it away. That's real. And, yes, you really can see it come into being in your life. You have what it takes to see those dreams come true because you have a limitless God living in you. He has given you all you need and made you all you need to be."

Then I'd get you a cookie too (because believe me, you'd feel like you need one by then), and we'd talk through all the fears, how it really can happen, what to do next.

You might ask me, "What makes God-sized dreams so important to you?"

I'd tell you that I've lived my share. Some have come true—like being a writer, counselor, life coach, and speaker. Others, like my desire for children, have led me to places of heartbreak and then healing without ever turning out the way I imagined. Through it all, the happy and the hard, I've discovered that the places I feel closest to Jesus, the moments when God is most real in my life, always seem to come when I'm on an adventure with him. And once you've learned that, you can't ever go back to life as you knew it. I'll share more about my God-sized dreams as we go along.

I'd also say that what I've experienced has been echoed by thousands of women on my blog, through emails and life coaching, at my church, and in many other ways. Do you feel like you're alone in your dream? You're not, my friend. I'm right beside you now on these pages. And because I'm passionate about God-sized dreamers, I also do e-coaching for women like you online (find out more at www.holleygerth.com). Many, many of your sisters are on this God-sized dream journey with you too. You'll even hear some of their stories in the following pages.

So consider this book that conversation we'd have over coffee or tea. What I've written is a gift from my heart to yours, from one dreamer to another. I believe with you, for you, and most of all—I believe in the God who lives within you.

You really are made for more.

And this is your time.

Right here, right now.

How Dreaming Begins

I sit in the backseat of a pickup truck with my nieces and nephews. Scrawny legs and arms restlessly swing back and forth as they try to pass the time. To distract them, I ask the question all adults do: "What do you want to be when you grow up?"

The answer comes swiftly and universally: "We want to work at Chuck E. Cheese's!" For those of you not familiar with Chuck E. Cheese's, it's an establishment full of pizza, games, and far too much sugar—the perfect spot to start your career, in the eyes of a six-year-old.

Fast-forward a few years and we're standing in the kitchen around the holidays. Those scrawny legs and arms have grown into tall teen bodies, and I check to see how the professional ambitions are going. "Do you still want to work at Chuck E. Cheese's when you grow up?"

I get laughs and quizzical looks as if I've gone crazy. "Aunt Holley!" they exclaim. "Why would we ever want to do that?"

When we start dreaming as children, it's a lot like practice. We learn to ride bicycles, and we also become more skilled at turning the wheels in our minds. We tell people we want to be astronauts or queens and to find ponies under our Christmas trees.

It's a fine line between reality and what's possible when we're children. Like for my nieces and nephews, most of those dreams disappear through the years, and that's okay. As we mature, so do our desires. Yet in those early dreams, we often find the seeds of the *something more* God has planted within us. If I'd asked you the same question I posed to my nieces and nephews, what would you have said?

(Note: Throughout the book you'll find interactive tools like the one below. If you'd like to download a printable version, go to the "Books & More" page at www.holleygerth.com. You can also download a printable version of the Go Deeper Guides that are at the end of each chapter.)

What were some of your childhood dreams?

I vividly remember perching on the edge of my parents' bed as a child. I squeezed my eyes tight, took a giant leap, and flapped my arms as hard as I could. Landing on the ground, I ran to my mom and dad to declare, "I flew!"

As I got older, I realized that as much as I felt like it was true, I hadn't actually become the world's first flying child that day.

"Flying is an impossible dream," some would say. Yet I have flown across the country and even across the world—many times.

Sure, as I grew up I realized I needed a plane to make the dream happen. But few things thrill me like staring out the window of a jet at twinkling lights below and thinking to myself, "I'm flying." I feel like that kid at the edge of the bed all over again.

Imagine I said, "I can't fly with my arms, so I'm not going to fly at all. What a silly dream. I need to grow up, face reality, and forget that ever even crossed my mind."

You'd probably say, "Holley, you might want to reconsider. Don't you ever want to go to Hawaii, visit Paris, or even just be able to visit your family without spending hours in the car? You're giving up so much!"

Yet we often do the same with our dreams. As children we let our imaginations go wild, and as time passes we begin to understand more of what's reality and what's fantasy. Rather than seeing those outlandish desires as a natural part of childhood, we convince ourselves that we're irresponsible dreamers. We need to settle down. Face the facts. Forget about flying and keep our feet on the ground.

Says who?

Who told you to stop dreaming? Maybe it was a teacher who told you to sit still in class and stop drawing those pictures. Maybe it was an overly cautious parent who wanted to keep you from getting hurt. Maybe it was the bully on the playground who yelled to the whole class that you were weird.

What if they were wrong?

Oh, of course there are dreams that we do need to let go. Like the Chuck E. Cheese ambitions of my nieces and nephews, sometimes a dream is more of a wish, and it blows away like a dandelion in the winds of time.

But if someone said or did something that made you stop dreaming altogether, then, my friend, I can assure you that wasn't from Jesus.

Dreaming is a core part of who we are. True, not all of our dreams come from God and not all of them are his will for our lives (more on that later), but the capacity to use our imaginations, to have visions, to nurture desires is inherent in who he has created us to be. "A longing fulfilled is a tree of life" (Prov. 13:12).

Dreams and desires propel us forward. In many ways, they keep us moving toward heaven—they don't allow us to get too comfortable here, to settle in ways and places God never intended.

As long as you are alive, God wants you to go further, dig deeper, and draw closer to him. And I believe dreams are one of the primary ways God makes that happen. *Every dream or desire you have that comes from God is an invitation for more intimacy with him.*

Did you catch that?

You can stop feeling guilty about dreaming and hoping.

And if life has diminished your capacity to dream, here's your permission to start again.

Really.

Five Lies That Keep Us from Dreaming

Ever since Eden, the enemy has come at us with a million different versions of the same question, "Did God really say . . . ?" And many times those questions are aimed squarely at our dreams.

Did God really say you have what it takes?

Did God really say that's what you're supposed to do?

When you follow your God-sized dreams, you'll face many external obstacles. But the biggest threats are from the inside. So let's start there.

Lie #1: "Dreaming Is Selfish"

She sits on the edge of her chair and stares at the corner of the room. I watch her fidget and run her fingers along the edge of her jeans. I can tell she's thinking of the husband and children and laundry waiting for her at home.

"I want to follow this dream," she says. "But it just feels so selfish."

From all the women I've talked to about God-sized dreams, this is the lie I hear most often. Women are a generous gender. We care deeply, passionately. We'd do anything for the ones we love. We serve selflessly. That is good, beautiful, and true.

But you matter too.

So do your dreams. The enemy knows that it's often one little word that can stop our dreaming in its tracks: *selfish*. We come to a screeching halt and say, "I'm not going within ten feet of that possibility." But if we tiptoe closer to that lie, we can see it for what it really is—a mirage.

Let me cup your lovely face in my hands and whisper this loud enough for your heart to hear: "Your dreams, your desires, your hopes are not selfish when they are from God's heart and in his hands."

"God is love" (1 John 4:16). Everything he does is loving. Everything he places within you is loving. That includes your dreams.

Now, if your dream is to run off to Tahiti with the pool boy and live on a two-hundred-foot yacht, then honey, that's a whole different story.

But if you have yielded to God and you have this nagging desire within you that just won't go away, then most likely it's from him. And if it is, then he has a way that you can live it out that isn't about selfishness but instead is about service.

Oh, the dream may look different than you imagined. You might be speaking at local women's ministry meetings instead of jetting across the country every weekend. But there is a way for that longing in your heart to be fulfilled that will be a blessing to those around you too.

The people in your life may not always like that you're following your dream. They may even whine about it from time to time. But not pleasing people isn't the same as being selfish. You don't have to make everyone in your life happy—the only thing you must do is be obedient.

Lie #2: "I Don't Have What It Takes"

She sits in the back row with me as the speaker takes the stage. Powerful words pour forth, and it's clear the women in the audience are touched. During the applause my friend leans over and says, "See, I could never speak. She's so much better than me."

It seems as soon as we give ourselves permission to dream, comparison is nipping at our heels. We look around and see others who are better, skinnier, more eloquent than us. Before we even get started, we disqualify ourselves. We vow to hold back until we're "as good as they are." Before we know it, time slips by and our dream still waits for its turn.

This lie is ultimately rooted in the belief that our God-sized dream is the same as someone else's. When we decide that's true, it means we're competitors because there aren't enough dreams to go around. But the reality is, even if someone else's dream looks, sounds, or even feels like yours—it's not the same.

God has a dream for you, your talents, your one life that has never been and never will be duplicated by anyone else.

He doesn't want you to be a "me too" when it comes to your dreams. He wants the one, original you whom he created to do exactly what he made you alone to do. No one else can fulfill your purpose. No one else can make that dream happen. There is no plan B for what God has destined to come into being through you.

It doesn't matter if you think you're not as good as someone else. You have what it takes to fulfill the dream God has for your life, and no one else does.

If the person you view as being the "top" in the area of your dreams were to trade places with you, it wouldn't work—even if it seemed like they were better at it than you. That's because God isn't interested in "better" or "the best." He can use sticks and stones to do his will if he wants! What God cares most about is

We're talking of God-sized dreams.

About how they are messy, imperfect, glorious, and flawed.

Because we are too.

And one phrase keeps reverberating through my being:

If not for grace . . .

If not for grace . . .

If not for grace, God-sized dreams would never come true.

Because I can tell you from experience . . .

You will cry at the wrong time.

You will say that awkward thing.

You will forget what to do in that most important moment.

And God, in his stubbornness, will carry on with his plan anyway.

You will fail at least once, and probably more.

You will think you are incapable.

And sometimes you will be.

But God, in his audacity, will use you anyway.

You will miss opportunities.

You will take steps you shouldn't.

You will walk through the wrong door and shut the right one.

And somehow, inexplicably, God will get you there anyway.

You will be hard to live with sometimes.

You will fall short.

You will forget to stand tall.

And God, unconcerned about what's cool, will say, "That one's mine" anyway.

You see, God-sized dreams don't make sense.

Not a bit.

Because they come from the heart of the One whose ways are higher than ours.

They flow from the One who stubbornly believes in grace.

If not for grace . . .

we wouldn't take a step

because it's grace that paves the road to God-sized dreams.

And we walk it, unworthy,

utterly broken,

and entirely loved!

your relationship with him, your obedience, your ability to hear his voice and say yes when he asks you to take a step of faith.

You are the only you we have. That means your God-sized dream either happens through you or not at all.

Lie #3: "It's Too Late"

She stands with a baby on her hip, and three others are causing chaos in the background. Above the noise she declares, "Well, I once had dreams, but now all I've got is diapers. It's too late for me." I've heard retired people, those with chronic illness, and many facing difficult circumstances say the same thing—that it's too late. Perhaps this is the hardest lie of all. It locks our dreams into a time bomb, and once we think it's exploded, it seems there's no picking up the pieces again.

It's true that our original vision may not come to pass. The "happily ever after" we pictured in our minds as little girls may have veered off course. But like I said before, I believe as long as we're alive, our dreams are too. God doesn't plant desires within our hearts to let them wither and die. Yes, they may be dormant for a season. And yes, when they finally push through the ground, they may look nothing like what we anticipated—but they're still possible.

I once knew a couple who longed to have children for years, but it never came to pass. The desire never went away, and in their sixties God called them to be "parents" to many children in a country far away. Now their family is bigger than they ever could have imagined. Like for Abraham and Sarah in the Old Testament, the answer to their prayers seemed a long time coming . . . but it did come. And that wouldn't have been possible unless they kept their hearts open to dreaming.

My grandpa Hollie (yes, I'm named after him) is ninety years old. Almost every time we're on the phone, he tells me of another place he'd like to visit. Then he finds a way to make it happen. He's an example to me that God decides when we're done. It's not up to us to say, "That dream is over. It's just not possible anymore." With God all things are possible (see Matt. 19:26).

It's only too late for our dreams when we decide to write "The End" on our stories and close the book. As an anonymous quote my mom has on her refrigerator reads, "Never place a period where God has placed a comma."

Lie #4: "I Don't Deserve to Dream"

The tears trickle down her face, and she reaches for a tissue. "But you don't understand," she says with a sigh. "I've messed up so much. The life I have now is a consequence of the choices I've made. I don't get to have the desires of my heart—I'm paying for what I've done."

I reach out my arms to her and try to wrap her up in words of grace too. "Your dreams aren't about you," I say. "They're about what God wants to do in his kingdom through you. And he'll use anyone—just look at some of the characters in the Bible! If adultery, murder, and deception didn't stop him, then what you've done isn't going to either!"

She laughs and looks up with a smile and perhaps just a bit of hope too.

Yes, you should pay for what you've done. So should I. But that's the beauty of the cross: Jesus took that payment for us. We may live with consequences, but we're not sentenced to a life of unfulfilled dreams and desires. Jesus said, "It is finished" on the cross so that we don't ever have to say the same in our lives. We are never finished—only fallen. If you've made mistakes, then do what you can to make them right, ask forgiveness, and get back up.

Listen closely, my friend. You have not been disqualified from dreaming. No matter what you've done. No matter what choices you've made. No matter what's in your past. Dreams are about the future. We can say these words with the apostle Paul, a man who had murder, persecuting Christians, and a long list of other sins in his past: "But one thing I do: Forgetting what is behind and straining toward what is ahead, I press on toward the goal to win the prize for which God has called me heavenward in Christ Jesus" (Phil. 3:13–14).

Right here, right now, take back your God-given permission to dream and to follow the desires of your heart.

Lie #5: "I Don't Have Time"

I bump into her in an aisle of the local grocery store. I ask, "How's that dream we talked about going?"

She brushes a stray hair from in front of her eyes and sighs. "I really want to move forward with it, but I'm just so busy. Maybe when things get back to normal." I nod my head with understanding since I've said the same thing many times too. And it can certainly be legitimate.

Yet at some point we have to decide that the time for our dream is now—no matter what. Because in today's world, normal never comes. There's always more to do, another "when I . . ." to check off the list, another urgent demand to be met.

If the enemy can't make us deny our dreams, then it seems his next tactic is to make us delay them. Yes, there are seasons for waiting and being still because that's what God has asked us to do. I'm not talking about those. I'm speaking of the seasons when we let procrastination get the best of us (and we all do sometimes). It's a great way to hold back the fear that inevitably comes when we actually pursue our dreams rather than just talking about them.

So, ladies, let's have a little heart-to-heart confession time. Because the truth is, as the old saying goes, "There is always enough time in our day to do God's will." If that dream in your heart really is from him and his timing is now, then somewhere in your schedule there's space to make it happen.

Hard? Always. But so is living with regret.

You don't have to pursue your dream perfectly. You only have to do what you can. Efforts that fall short of your expectations are still always better than none at all. God can fill in the gaps.

Only you know if this really is the season for your dream, and only you can decide to truly pursue it. I love the biblical phrase "for such a time as this" (Esther 4:14) because it says so much about right here, right now. It's not "for such a time as then" or "for such a time as that." It speaks to today and the moments passing us by that will not come again.

You have time. I have time.

If it's not the season for your dream, then embrace that and focus on what God has in front of you now. That's honorable and faith-filled too.

But if it's your moment to take that step, make that leap, birth that dream, then go for it with all your heart and don't let anything or anyone block your way (or your schedule).

The Truth That Sets Us Free to Dream

She walks through the door with a smile on her face. It seems like she's standing a bit taller, moving a bit faster, glowing with an inner light. "The lies were so loud," she confesses. "But I just kept pressing in to Jesus until his voice was even louder."

The lies don't ever go away. Every step of your dream, they will chase you. It doesn't mean that you're not spiritual enough or you're on the wrong path. It just means that "our struggle is not against flesh and blood, but against the rulers, against the authorities, against the powers of this dark world and against the spiritual forces of evil in the heavenly realms" (Eph. 6:12). You are in a battle—expect opposition.

But remember this too: You have already been promised victory. Nothing can separate you from God's love. And when you're following hard after his heart, nothing can separate you from his will either.

As I write this, I'm looking at a small print by Dee at Red Letter Words that says, "She knew that many were the plans in her heart but that God's purpose would prevail" (paraphrased from Prov. 19:21). I need that plaque every single day. It reminds me that my role isn't results—it's obedience. It's the willingness to take the risks and let God do the rest.

You, my friend, are a dreamer. Whether you know it or not. Whether you're at the beginning of your journey or sitting exhausted in the Promised Land after battling to possess it.

You, my friend, are an Esther—chosen and placed in your generation *for such a time as this*. Your life matters even more than you know, and you are making a difference even more than you see.

You, my friend, are a warrior. Every day you dare to dream, you fight back the darkness and add a little more light to the world. When you keep your heart open, the kingdom wins.

And you, my friend, are on an adventure that's going to take you to places beyond what you could have even imagined. Places with joy, tears, glory, grace, and most of all, *more of Jesus* with each step you take.

The "more" your heart has always hoped for is what God has wanted to give you all along.

So let's get going.

Go Deeper Guide

(Download a printable version with lines for writing at www.holleygerth.com on the "Books & More" page.)

1. What were some of your childhood dreams?
2. What messages were given to you about dreaming (both positive and negative) as you were growing up?
3. "Every dream or desire you have that comes from God is an invitation for more intimacy with him." Do you agree or disagree with this statement? Why?
4. What's one of your God-sized dreams?
5. Which of the lies listed in this chapter did you most identify with? What's the truth God wants to speak to your heart instead?
6. "Our struggle is not against flesh and blood, but against the rulers, against the authorities, against the powers of this dark world and against the spiritual forces of evil in the heavenly realms" (Eph. 6:12). What's one thing standing between you and the dream God has placed in your heart right now? What's a way to overcome it?
7. Think of someone in your life who is pursuing a God-sized dream. What's their story? What have you learned from them?

— *Dream It. Do It.* —

Create a vision board that expresses your God-sized dream visually. You can use photos, clippings from magazines, or images you find online. It can be any size or shape—just as long as it inspires you as you look at it.

2

You Might Have a **God-Sized Dream** If . . .

"But how do I know it's not just me? What if I'm just making this up?"

These are the most common questions I hear about God-sized dreams and chasing "more" in our lives. We want to please God. We want to be purposeful. So we worry the whisper within our hearts is somehow not really from him after all.

Is there a way to be sure?

Perhaps not 100 percent. But after talking with thousands of women about their God-sized dreams, I've found there do seem to be some filters you can put yours through to be more certain than before.

You Might Have a God-Sized Dream If It Fits with Your Strengths

She describes the new opportunity that has suddenly appeared in her life. "I really want to do this, but I'm just not sure. What should I think about when I make this decision?" she asks.

I respond, "Well, first let's look at who you are and how well this fits with the way God has made you."

"Really?" she replies. "I always thought about the external aspects—pay, location, opportunities for advancement—but not about the internal ones like who I am. That sounds better!"

The God-sized dreams in our lives usually fit pretty tightly with who he made us to be. Just think of Jesus telling Peter, "Don't be afraid; from now on you will fish for people" (Luke 5:10). What was his current occupation? Fishing. Yes, Peter applied his skills in a completely new way on a totally different adventure, but the core characteristics (tenacity, risk taking, making it through storms) would serve him well when he answered yes to this God-sized dream.

You are who you are for a reason. God could have designed you in any way that he wanted. After all, he spoke the world into being. Customizing you wasn't a challenge. So why would he create you in a way that *didn't* match up with the biggest dreams he has for your life?

One of the myths that tends to derail us from our dreams is the idea that to truly be spiritual we shouldn't really enjoy what we're called to do. We sit in church and hope God doesn't "call me to a poor tribe in Africa." Well, most likely that isn't going to happen. And if it does, you're probably the kid who sat enraptured by the stories of overseas missions in Sunday school, who loved learning about different cultures, who had a knack for making friends in unlikely places. The apostles weren't the only ones whose callings remained consistent with how they were created.

David the shepherd went on to guide the flock of God's people.

Saul, a zealous leader for the Jews, turned into Paul, a zealous leader for Jesus.

Moses, raised in the house of Pharaoh, eventually stood before royalty and rescued the Israelites.

Why would God be motivated to put you in a position where the way he wired you isn't utilized?

Your strengths aren't always arrows pointing directly to your God-sized dreams, but many times that is the case. If you read my first book, *You're Already Amazing*, then you should already be familiar with your strengths. If not, then let's take a quick look again here. Even if you have done this work already, it can be helpful to review it again.

A strength is a personal characteristic that can be used on behalf of God in service to others. Usually they're present throughout our lives but can be enhanced through experience or training. Strengths are part of *who we are* while skills are more about *what we do.*

Find Your Strengths: 5 Minutes

Circle three strengths that apply to you.

- Adventurous
- Athletic
- Brave
- Calm
- Capable
- Caring
- Cheerful
- Considerate
- Courageous
- Creative
- Dedicated
- Determined
- Devoted
- Easygoing
- Efficient
- Encouraging
- Energetic
- Fair
- Flexible
- Forgiving
- Friendly
- Frugal
- Funny
- Gentle
- Gracious
- Hardworking
- Helpful
- Honest
- Hospitable
- Imaginative
- Intelligent
- Kind
- Loving
- Loyal
- Mature
- Organized
- Positive
- Protective
- Reflective
- Reliable
- Resilient
- Resourceful
- Responsible
- Sensitive
- Servant-hearted
- Spontaneous
- Supportive
- Talented
- Thoughtful
- Trustworthy
- Warm
- Wise
- *Add your own . . .*

If you're still wondering if the words you circled are strengths, then you can put them through the STRENGTH test:

Service	*Does it help me serve God and others?*
Time	*Has it been present throughout much of my life?*
Relationships	*Do others see this?*
Energy	*Do I feel energized when I'm living this way?*
Natural	*Does this come naturally to me most of the time? Or do I know God has intentionally developed this in me even though it doesn't?*
Glory	*Does God ultimately get the glory from it?*
Trials	*Even in hard times, does it usually come through somehow?*
Heart	*Does this really feel like a core part of who I am?*

What are the parts of who you are that consistently bring God glory and bless others? What are the moments in your day when you find yourself saying, "This is why I'm on earth"? In the busyness of life, we can miss those clues or dismiss them as not being valid. We tell ourselves that surely a God-sized dream has to be more spiritual, be harder, or resemble what our neighbor is doing.

But like we talked about earlier, God-sized dreams aren't one size fits all. You and your God-sized dream are perfectly paired by the One who created you both.

You Might Have a God-Sized Dream If Your Skills and Experiences Have Prepared You for It

She describes her life to me—work, family, church. At the end I smile and say, "You always find a way to teach wherever you are, don't you?" She pauses and then softly laughs. "Yes, I guess I do! So starting a new class for pregnant teen moms makes a whole lot of sense, doesn't it?"

Just as God crafts who we are in specific ways, he also gives us certain skills and experiences. Think of them as practice for your dream. They may not be exactly the same. For example, the woman above didn't have a career as a teacher, but she found herself stepping into that role every chance she got. The skills and experiences she gained as she did so provided preparation for the God-sized dream she was now considering.

When we hear Sunday school stories, they often begin at the "big moment" of a hero's life. Yet when we look back over his or her life, it becomes clear that God has been laying the groundwork for years. For example, we've all heard of how God spoke to Moses from a burning bush in the desert and asked him to lead the people of Israel out of slavery. It seems that's where the story begins. But by that time Moses is quite old! What has he spent his life doing so far? He grew up in Pharaoh's household and then he became a shepherd—both involved skills and experiences that would serve him well in this new mission.

A skill is a strength expressed in a specific way that builds up others and benefits the kingdom.

What are some of the skills you consistently use?

Find Your Skills: 5 Minutes

Circle three skills that apply to you.

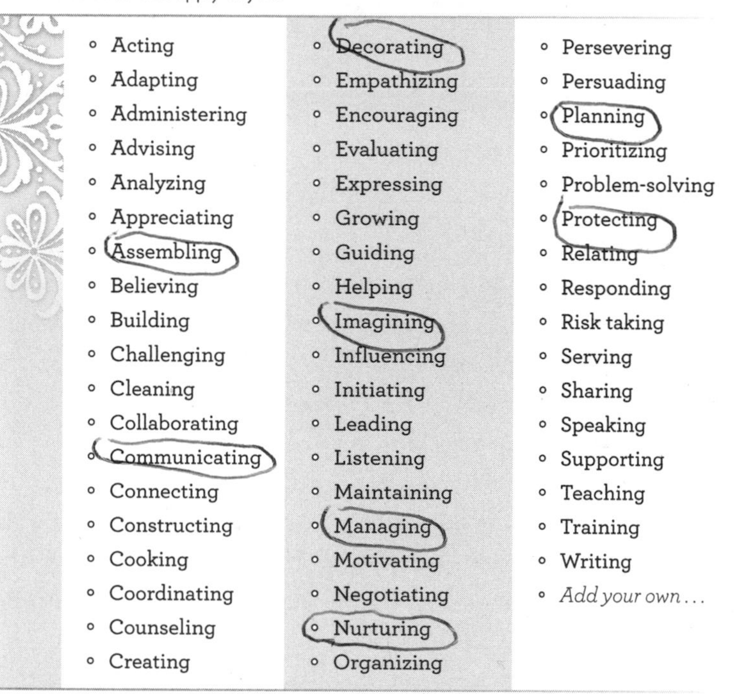

- Acting
- Adapting
- Administering
- Advising
- Analyzing
- Appreciating
- Assembling
- Believing
- Building
- Challenging
- Cleaning
- Collaborating
- Communicating
- Connecting
- Constructing
- Cooking
- Coordinating
- Counseling
- Creating
- Decorating
- Empathizing
- Encouraging
- Evaluating
- Expressing
- Growing
- Guiding
- Helping
- Imagining
- Influencing
- Initiating
- Leading
- Listening
- Maintaining
- Managing
- Motivating
- Negotiating
- Nurturing
- Organizing
- Persevering
- Persuading
- Planning
- Prioritizing
- Problem-solving
- Protecting
- Relating
- Responding
- Risk taking
- Serving
- Sharing
- Speaking
- Supporting
- Teaching
- Training
- Writing
- *Add your own . . .*

Whatever skills you use that seem to be lining up with your God-sized dreams are the areas where you should continue seeking to grow. Yes, we have some natural ability in these areas, but research has shown that practice, education, and experience help us hone our skills so that we can do more than just use them—we can master them. You have been entrusted with certain ways of making a difference in the world, and it's up to you to make the most of them during your time on earth.

Our experiences allow us to apply our strengths and skills. They also show us more about what we're *not* called to do. What are some of the significant experiences in your life that have brought you to this God-sized dream? What do they tell you about your God-sized dreams? Write your answer below (examples: education, jobs, significant turning points, lessons learned).

When we have a God-sized dream on our hearts, it can be easy to hurry past where we are now. What we're doing may seem like a "waste of time" when we can see the vision ahead so clearly. Yet where you are today may be exactly the training you need for the place where God wants to take you tomorrow.

If you think, "I don't have any skills or experiences related to this dream," then take some time to consider whether it's wise to get some before you step into this new phase. Yes, there are times when God wants us to simply go for it, but more often, he prepares us for what's ahead.

Most likely you have already been doing something related to your dream. Maybe in a different place. Maybe in a different way. Maybe with different people. Look for the threads of God's work in your life and how he's tying them together into your dream.

You Might Have a God-Sized Dream If You Can't Think about Anything Else

She rubs the sleep from her eyes, yawns widely, and grins. "I had a new idea last night, and I got so excited I could hardly sleep!"

"Tell me all about it," I say with a smile.

God-sized dreams make their way into our hearts, homes, nights, and every other area. Sometimes they feel like an insistent knocking on a door within us. We can't get any rest until we let them inside.

While this can be a bit bothersome at times, it's also a tremendous gift. God-sized dreams take lots of energy. And energy comes from passion. This isn't a feeling of "Well, one day I might want to. . . ." My friend and fellow writer Lisa-Jo Baker described it this way in a conversation once: "I wake up every morning, and it's like Jesus has his hand on the back of my neck, and he's gently pushing me forward and saying, 'Go, girl, *go*.'"

We all have ideas that cross our minds. But this is much deeper, wilder. It doesn't feel like we have a choice but rather that *we have been chosen*. Someone is calling our name deep inside, and ignoring that voice is almost impossible.

Yes, sometimes we may bury that calling for a season or try to walk away. But in the quiet moments, it keeps coming back. It pulls at us and demands our attention. Few places in life are as miserable as where you find yourself when you are actively running away from your God-sized dream. Remember Jonah? Called to preach in Nineveh, he hightails it out of town in a different direction. He winds up in the belly of a whale for three days. We may not find ourselves in such extreme circumstances, but the feeling of discomfort is one to which anyone who has tried to sidestep a dream can relate.

Why are God-sized dreams so compelling? Because we powerfully experience God's presence in our lives through them. It's not about the destination. It's not what we will get if we complete the dream. It's about a relationship.

As the Israelites crossed the desert, the cloud of God's presence hovered above the tabernacle and led them along the way. When the cloud moved, they moved. When the cloud stayed, they stayed.

If God is calling you to a dream, then that's where his presence is in your life. You are not being drawn to the dream—you are being drawn to the giver of it.

The pursuit of any God-sized dream is ultimately the pursuit of the One who placed it within you. It's like a homing beacon for your heart.

You Might Have a God-Sized Dream If You're Scared Silly

She sends me an email that says, "I want to move forward but I'm totally scared. Maybe I should wait until I feel a bit more courageous."

I click the keys in response. "Friend, if this is what God is calling you to, then do it now. The fear is never going away."

As human beings, we were wired by God in a wonderful way for survival. Our bodies automatically tell us, "If there's a threat, then you should fight it or avoid it." In most cases, that works really well. But when it comes to God-sized dreams, it's very different. We'll spend a whole chapter on fear later, but for now I just want to dispel the myth that fear means your dream isn't from God. You are human, and when you decide to take a risk (and every dream is a risk), then you will always feel fear. You have a choice about what to do in response to that fear, but feeling it in the first place is often more of a confirmation of your dream than a sign you should walk away from it.

I would even take it a step further and say that if you don't feel any fear at all, then it's probably not a God-sized dream. Our God is big, wild, and far beyond our understanding and limits. He tells us, "My thoughts are not your thoughts, neither are your ways my ways" (Isa. 55:8). That means whenever he asks us to do something, it is almost always out of our comfort zones. It usually doesn't make sense ("Hey, Noah, build an ark"). It most often involves a lot of change ("Hey, disciples, leave everything you know and follow me"). It always stretches our faith ("Hey, Esther, go before the king to save your people even though it may cost your life").

What makes you afraid? I don't mean the "Eek! A spider!" kind of fear. I mean the idea that pops into your mind that makes your heart start to pound and your skin begin to sweat, *and yet* you are strangely drawn to it anyway. That just might be your God-sized dream.

The moment that changes everything is when we decide to fear God more than we fear what may happen.

You Might Have a God-Sized Dream If People Think You're Crazy

My cell phone rings. "Can you meet me for dinner? I just shared my idea, and everyone looked at me like I'm out of my mind. I need some encouragement!"

I reply, "Sounds like it went great! I'll tell you why when we get to the restaurant."

When our heart beats with passion for an idea, we quickly assume that everyone else feels the same way. We have a vision and we believe that all those around us should be able to see it just as clearly as we do.

At one point in my life, I had a God-sized dream that I longed to bring into reality. I needed an entire team of people to get on board in order for that to happen. I would share a few sentences in a meeting and get blank stares. I felt frustrated and alone. My life coach, Denise Martin, gently corrected me. "Holley, they can't see what you do. You are the vision carrier. You have to share it with them in a way they can understand. Don't assume that they have this dream too. God has given it to you." When she said those words to me, a lightbulb went on inside. I hadn't been effectively communicating because I thought that everyone else must know and see what I did. Once I changed my approach, people did get on board—although throughout the process I still remained the one with the most passion. That didn't mean I failed. It simply meant God had entrusted that particular dream *to me*.

If you have a God-sized dream, it's natural to want everyone around you to "get it" in the same way, right away. But that probably isn't going to happen. If your idea takes some explaining, that's a good sign. As we talked about before, God's thoughts are not our thoughts. God-sized dreams often don't make sense in our world.

Ask yourself, "Who has to be completely on board with this dream?" This should be a *very* small list. Carefully and intentionally communicate the dream to these people. Then go ahead and let everyone else think you're crazy. You don't need buy-in from all your co-workers, your entire Bible study, your high school friends on Facebook, and the checkout girl at the grocery store. Sometimes we delay our dreams because we think that everyone's approval is confirmation. (*Psst—it's not.*)

If you have prayed, planned, and sought wise counsel from a small group of people in your life, then go ahead and move forward. Expect the blank stares. Anticipate the questioning of your sanity or stability. Be prepared for the questions—and even opposition. Then smile, nod, and move ahead anyway. It's not your job to make your God-sized dream make sense to everyone. They'll see it soon enough when God brings it into being.

You Might Have a God-Sized Dream If It's Bigger Than You Are

"I just have this sense that it's not really about me at all," she says softly. "I get to play a part, but I'm not the main character in this story."

We eat, sleep, breathe our God-sized dreams, and yet in many ways they have very little to do with us. As Rick Warren famously said at the beginning of *The Purpose Driven Life*, "It's not about you."[1]

God-sized dreams are not about your personal fulfillment.

God-sized dreams are not about making you happy.

God-sized dreams are not about filling the empty spaces in your soul.

Yes, all along the way you will be tempted to make your dream about those things. That's just part of being human. But ultimately you know that the calling in your soul is about more, so much more than anything you might hope to gain from it.

If those are the *only* reasons you're pursuing the dream, then it's time to hit the Pause button. Sometimes what we think are God-sized dreams are actually neon signs flashing an unmet need in our lives. Let me tell you a secret: *your dream will not fill you up inside*. Yes, there will be some wonderful moments. Yes, there will be joy along the way. But it will also be hard, even exhausting, and push you to your limits at times.

If you're thinking, "When I _______ (fill in the blank with your dream here), then I will be _______ (fill in the blank with your unmet need here, such as 'happy')," then you may have some more work to do within your heart. Because your dream is not about you.

It's about the God who gave it to you.

It's about the kingdom he's building in this world.

It's about the body of Christ.

His plan is for you to benefit as well—everything he does is for your good. But the dreams he places within our hearts are always about a bigger picture, the grander story he's writing all through history.

If your dream sometimes makes you feel very small, that's a good thing. God-sized dreams can feel like gazing up at the stars at night. We are reminded that in this great big universe, our little world is just one piece of an endless, eternal puzzle.

The good news is that you don't have to be big to have God-sized dreams, because in him you are enough. It's not the size of the dream or dreamer that matters. Those stars that make us feel small were spoken into being by the One who walks beside you, lives within you, calls your name, and dares you to dream beyond yourself.

You Might Have a God-Sized Dream If It Aligns with God's Purposes

She sets the Bible on the couch and leans back. "I know we're studying something else, but all I can see when I look in here is my God-sized dream!"

We've been using the word *if* to talk about these possibilities. But when it comes to this one, it's a must. God-sized dreams always align with his purposes. And Scripture shows us what those are and how we can live them out in our generation.

Does it talk about your dream specifically? Probably not. You're not going to find a page that says, "I want you to open a cozy bakery so that you can feed the hungry hearts of women at the same time you're feeding their bodies too." But when we look at the broader principles that dream embodies—service, reaching out, loving God and people—then it clearly can be something that advances the kingdom of God.

Not all God-sized dreams are super-spiritual. Many are practical. Some are loud and out in the open. Others are quiet and hidden. Yours might keep you at home or send you to the farthest corner of the earth. It may involve face-to-face interactions or clicking the keys on your computer.

Just look around you. Creation is full of variety, and each new dream is another aspect of what God is expressing in the world. Yet all those different expressions point back to the same purposes, the same desires of his heart.

God-sized dreams always align biblically. If your desire takes you outside the boundaries God has set, then it's not from him. But within those boundaries, we have so much freedom! Jesus tells a parable of a master who leaves his servants in charge of different amounts of "talents," which was the word for money in those days (see Matt. 25:14–30). You're probably familiar with how all three use what they've been given differently and get varying responses from the master as a result. What intrigues me about this story is that the master doesn't give specific instructions. He doesn't leave a detailed to-do list.

Sometimes we want to know exactly what God wants us to do before we move ahead with a dream. And yes, he does promise to guide us through his Holy Spirit. Yet there also seems to be an element of letting us choose how we will invest our lives. He has given you certain things—strengths, skills, experiences. What will you do with them? As long as what we do honors the Master, then most likely we have the freedom to pursue it.

If we make the wrong decision, there is grace and God is able to redirect as well as redeem. What's more dangerous is doing nothing at all, as the third servant who buries his talents quickly learns upon the master's return. Doing nothing isn't the safest or most godly option. God never rebukes anyone in Scripture for making a mistake when their sincere desire is to please him.

If what you long to do fits with what God wants too, then you have freedom to move forward in faith. He will get you where he wants you to go in the end—even if you take a few detours along the way.

You Might Have a God-Sized Dream If It's Harder Than You Thought It Would Be

She sighs. "I know this is what God wanted me to do. But nothing is turning out the way I imagined. Did I mess up?"

I give her a hug and say into her ear, "You, brave and beautiful girl, are right where you should be."

When we first discover our God-sized dream, all we can see is the perfect vision, the desired reality. We don't know about the desert in between where we are and the Promised Land. It catches us by surprise when there are delays, difficulties, obstacles to overcome. This is where most God-sized dreams fall by the wayside. When we hit the hard part, we want a fresh start. But there will *always* be challenges.

We're living out our dreams in an imperfect, fallen world and connecting with imperfect, fallen people along the way (including ourselves). Something is bound to go wrong. We're going to goof up. The plans we so meticulously created will sometimes not come to pass. *And that's okay.*

If you're in a place where it feels like what you've undertaken is much harder than you imagined, take heart. If God has called you to this, then he will get you through it. Here's a secret: *God-sized*

For such a time as this . . .

You're here, now, in this moment, and it will never come again.

For such a time as this . . .

You're changing diapers, tying the shoelaces of the future, growing the seeds of strong faith.

For such a time as this . . .

You're working in that office, speaking up in that meeting, doing what you do with excellence.

For such a time as this . . .

You're reaching out a helping hand, taking time to listen, brightening someone's day.

For such a time as this . . .

You are wherever you are, doing whatever you do, and it matters more than you know.

So keep it up, friend.

You really are making a difference.

dreams are invincible when we're obedient. He always wins in the end. Does that mean the result will look like what we had in mind at the beginning? Most likely not. But whatever purpose God has for your dream, he will bring to pass. *Your job is to not quit no matter what happens.* God will take care of the rest.

You Might Have a God-Sized Dream If It Leads to Joy

She's talking so fast I can hardly understand her. "We did it!" she declares. "After all that time and struggle, it actually happened!"

I clap my hands and we clink our coffee cups together in victory. *At last.*

Yes, God-sized dreams are hard. But they are also full of joy. Not the "everything is sunshine and roses" kind of happy but the deep satisfaction that comes from knowing you're doing what you're called to do.

When you make it to the Promised Land, there's simply nothing like it in the whole wide world. It makes everything—all the trials, detours, hard moments—fade into the background. You are here. You finished well. You completed the task.

There's joy along the way too. You'll see God coming through in ways you never could have imagined. You'll find out you're stronger than you ever thought possible. You'll see you're loved and supported more than you could have known.

Your God-sized dream is meant to bring your soul joy. It's intended to be a place where you experience deep intimacy with God and rejoice with him.

If you don't ever feel joy when pursuing your dream, then it may be that another motivation is actually prompting you to move forward. When we try to use our dreams to get rid of our insecurity, to earn love, or to meet needs in a way God never intended, then we don't feel joy—we feel desperation, hopelessness, and endless frustration. God will not let us be satisfied with anything but him. If there's no joy in your dream, ask him what your heart is really looking for instead.

When those times of joy do come, it's important to celebrate them. Those of us who are dreamers can rush on to the next adventure so quickly. But there's time for stopping, savoring, looking back on the journey, and reveling in what God has done in and through you.

God-sized dreams lead us to joy—and to the Giver of it.

Final Thoughts

God-sized dreams are mysterious. We catch a glimpse of where we're headed only to have the vision disappear like a mist on an early morning. God-sized dreams don't cooperate with checklists or agendas. They defy our timing and often our logic. The more we seek to control them, the quicker they slip beyond our grasp.

And yet we can't let them go. We're compelled to continue the pursuit.

I believe God lets it be that way, even makes it that way, because it draws us closer to him. Our dreams may be elusive, but he is ever-present. Our dreams may challenge our sense of safety, but he is our ultimate security. Our dreams may catch our interest, but he's the One who relentlessly chases our hearts.

You don't have to be sure about your dream before you move forward. You only have to be certain of the One who is whispering to you that it's time to come with him to a new place. Just take the next step. And then another.

Do you really have a God-sized dream?

Only God knows.

And sometimes the only way you'll know is to go with him.

It turns out most dreams aren't delivered to our door—they're discovered along the way.

Go Deeper Guide

(Download a printable version with lines for writing at www.holley gerth.com on the "Books & More" page.)

1. What are three of your strengths?
2. What are three of your skills?
3. Describe a moment in your life when you found yourself saying, "This is why I'm on earth."
4. Draw a time line of your life showing significant experiences that have helped bring you to where you are now.
5. What else might you need to do to prepare for the God-sized dream in your life?
6. Which of the "You might have a God-sized dream if . . ." statements from this chapter did you identify with most? Why?
7. "The joy of the LORD is your strength" (Neh. 8:10). What brings you joy, energizes you, and makes you feel closest to God? How is that a part of your God-sized dreams?

Dream It. Do It.

Sometimes those around us can see our strengths more clearly than we do because we tend to be so hard on ourselves. This week ask at least one other person in your life to share three strengths they see in you. You can do so face-to-face, on the phone, or through email.

3

The **Heart** of a Dreamer

I've met thousands of dreamers. Some are so quiet you can barely hear them in a crowded room. Some are so loud that as soon as they speak, everyone turns their way. Some are young, just starting the journey of their lives. Others have experienced decades of dreaming and are looking forward to leaving a legacy. Some are stay-at-home moms. Others are world-traveling businesswomen. Some don't wear makeup and love the rugged outdoors. Others have every nail done to perfection and think a day at the spa is the ultimate adventure. Some are right-brained, creative types. Others are left-brained, practical thinkers. Dreamers show up in every personality profile, economic level, geographic location, and every other variable you can imagine.

God loves variety.

And yet after meeting all of these dreamers, all of these wonderful women, I've noticed one aspect of who they are is remarkably the same.

Their hearts.

I have a strong feeling that if you've made it this far in this book, your heart is much the same too. So let's talk about you, dear dreamer, and what lies within you that makes you so different and yet so similar to many of your sisters.

God-Sized Dreamers Are Faithful Where They Are

In the Old Testament, God sent the prophet Samuel to anoint a new king (see 1 Sam. 16:1–13). Samuel arrived at a household with lots of sons. Good-looking ones. Tall ones. Impressive ones. But as each passed by, Samuel sensed that he had not yet found the one God sent him for. "Don't you have any more sons?" he asked. The father was dismissive. "Oh yeah, there's one more. But he's the youngest. Not even worth meeting. He's out in the fields with the sheep." Samuel demanded that the final son be brought, and it turned out he was God's choice all along. The shepherd boy David became the king. And God showed us this truth: "People look at the outward appearance, but the LORD looks at the heart" (1 Sam. 16:7).

David, the overlooked one, captured the gaze of God. Under seas of stars, out in the desert with no one around but a few sheep, he learned to pray, be brave, and dream with God. I wonder if he had any sense on those starry nights of what was coming, what God was preparing him for in the vastness of that quiet place. He learned to be faithful right where God had him, and that enabled God to place him exactly where he was supposed to be.

Where are you today?

Maybe you're in a place where it seems no one sees you and it feels like what you do doesn't matter. Maybe you feel like your potential isn't being used. What are you doing taking care of a few sheep when you sense inside that you're made for so much more? But you're being faithful anyway. You're serving, learning, loving, growing.

You aren't settling for the status quo, and yet you are choosing to thrive where you are today as well. Dreams can be seductive. They can make us trade our today for an unknown future. They can turn our thoughts away from what's right in front of us.

But not you. You're a God-sized dreamer, and that means you can make a difference anywhere. When Jesus said, "Whoever can be trusted with very little can also be trusted with much" (Luke 16:10), he meant folks like you. Listen, my friend, you are seen. You are watched by the One who spoke the world into being, who numbers every hair on your head and knows each care in your heart. If all those details matter to him, don't you think what you're doing right here, right now does too?

What you're doing isn't small if it's what God has for you. It's big. And it just may lead to something even bigger.

Make the most of where you are right now. Give everything you have. God has so much in store for you. And he has so much for you right here too.

You are a God-sized dreamer, and you are faithful right where you are. In case you haven't heard it lately, thank you. Thank you for what you do. Especially when it seems no one sees. Especially when you wonder if it matters at all. It does. And you do too.

Hello, friend!

I'm thinking of you this morning, wherever you are, and of the difference you're making.

You might think it's small.

You might think no one really sees.

You might think you should do something bigger, better, more spiritual.

But lean in and listen closely . . .

The best gift you can offer this world is Jesus in you.

And that's what you're doing—

just putting messy, glorious, imperfect, made-new you out there.

In your home, your family, your office, your community, your world.

We'd miss you if you weren't there. It just wouldn't be the same. And no one could take your place.

So keep it up, my friend. Keep giving and loving and living right where you are.

And for this moment, you can make it the very best place to be.

God-Sized Dreamers Keep Their Hearts Open

I flip on the television and yet another tale of woe spills into the living room. I see crossed arms, bitter faces, sharp glances that cut like swords. If I could peer into these hearts, I would most likely see a Closed sign hanging on the door.

I switch to another channel in time to catch the story of a woman in her eighties. She tells of a hard life, deep needs, hurts that would stop many of us in our tracks. But instead she beams. She tells of God's goodness and of her dream. She's feeding 150 people a day with what she's prepared with her two hands. And what she'd love more than anything in the world is to be able to do so for twice as many. The sign on her heart says Open in neon, glittering joy.

"In this world you will have trouble," said Jesus (John 16:33). And we do. No one escapes this life without times when tears slip down our cheeks and hope flees from our hearts. We all face loss, disappointment, and failure. That's why Jesus followed those words with three more: "But take heart!" In other words, keep the Open sign up no matter what. Don't let this world make you shut down and lock up what you're meant to share.

If you're a God-sized dreamer, that's the choice you've made. Maybe no one has ever said this to you, but I want to do so now:

If you have gone through hurts in this life and you have kept your heart open, then you are a remarkable person. And if you are reading this book and daring to still dream, then that's exactly what you've done. You are brave, strong, and beautiful. You have made a choice that few do. In the face of difficulties, you have managed to guard what matters most and to press ahead with a resilience that makes you a force to be reckoned with for the kingdom. Thank you for making that choice. Thank you for keeping your heart open. The world needs more people like you.

It's easy to decide to look out for number one. It's easy to push aside our dreams and settle for what's safest. It's easy to plaster a smile on our faces and never let anyone really get close to us. But it's hard to keep your heart open for a lifetime. It's hard to really let love be part of who you are each day. It's hard to keep risking, hoping, and praying even in the face of the impossible.

You might do all of those things without pausing to consider what a miracle it is that you do. It's not "normal" to live that way. In our world, it's much more common to close down and become cold, cynical, and bitter.

You are a light, my friend. Because when your heart is open, it's Jesus who shines out. And that glow illuminates the path to the dreams he's given you too.

God-Sized Dreamers Encourage Others

Caught up in the moment, she didn't notice the little girl behind her. As the woman's hands moved skillfully to combine flour, sugar, and eggs into a delicious confection, small eyes watched and little hands mixed the same invisible ingredients in a toy bowl. Years later, that little girl now grown would stand at her kitchen counter and think of the woman who inspired her to learn to cook.

Who's watching you?

If you're a dreamer, I can guarantee there are eyes on you. You may not see them, you may not even know, but you are encouraging and inspiring someone. In a world where dreamers are rare, you stand out whether you want to or not. You help others to listen harder to Jesus, to take leaps of faith, to live with passion.

You do this without words by the choices you make, the desires you pursue, the joy on your face.

Maybe you do the same with words too. I wouldn't be surprised a bit to learn that you have the spiritual gift of encouragement. Many dreamers do. If so, you're probably verbally helping others along. You cheer them up, cheer them on, and help them take another step when they feel like they want to quit. You notice the desires of their hearts, and you care about seeing them come true. God-sized dreaming is contagious, and you'd love for everyone around you to catch it.

You may think, "Oh, that's just who I am. And everyone else is like that too." Listen here, girl: you offer a rare gift to the world by being an encourager. Kind words are becoming an endangered species. A friend who will rejoice in your successes as much as her own is a treasure indeed. A woman who will say, "Yes, with God you can do this" is a beautiful and hard-to-find wonder.

Being a God-sized dreamer isn't just beneficial to you. It makes a difference to so many around you too. Meredith marketing group did an intriguing study about "Gamma Women."[2] They explain that there's a shift in our society from "Alpha Women" (think prom queen) to "Gamma Women" (think Miss Congeniality). Rather than seeking to try to climb the ladder, Gammas are the hub in a center of relationships. They influence by loving, not by leaping to the top. When they experience success, they take others with them each step of the way. Does that sound like you? I imagine it does. I think all God-sized dreamers are Gammas.

You encourage others. You do so through your life, through your words, through the passion you show in pursuing your dreams. The word *encourage* actually means to give someone courage. When you're a God-sized dreamer, that's exactly what you do. When you take risks, get up from failures, seek God even when it's hard, and eventually make it to the Promised Land, you make others want to do the same.

Someone is watching you today.

God is too.

And I've got a feeling there's a lot of joy happening as they do.

God-Sized Dreamers Are Positive People

We peer at the glasses on the dinner table. In the middle of a lively conversation, the old question has come up: "Do you see the glass as half full or half empty?" One responder adds a new twist: "I don't think it's about the glass at all but instead who is filling it."

Ah, I thought. *That sounds like a God-sized dreamer.*

God-sized dreamers aren't fixated on the glass. Reality is only a part of the equation for them. What matters most is the potential—and the limitless God who lives within them.

That means God-sized dreamers can be optimists. Not the pie-in-the-sky-everything-is-perfect kind. Not the slap-on-a-silly-grin type. I mean *true optimists*. The kind who can maintain a realistic, resilient belief even in the middle of difficult circumstances.

You are one of those people. You may even have had others tease you a bit about it. But let me tell you, being a true optimist in the world today is no small feat. Negativity is far easier than perseverance. Criticism is simpler than encouragement. Saying the world is going to end can be far more convenient than daring to make a difference in it.

That doesn't mean you believe life is all sunshine and roses. You've seen your share of hard times. You can bet there are more to come. But in the middle of it all, you keep holding on to the

God who will not let you go. You trust that he will come through for you. You don't let the embers of your dreams die but instead fan them into flame again and again.

Optimism doesn't come naturally to any of us. We're simply not wired that way. If you choose to focus on what is good, true, and lovely, then you've made a deliberate, difficult choice to do so. Others may think that you're one of those "naturally happy" people, but I imagine underneath it I would find some serious faith backed up by hard work and self-control.

Thank you for being a true optimist. Thank you for continuing to believe even in the face of doubt, criticism, or discouragement. Thank you for not sitting in the dark cave of despair but instead choosing to mine all of the diamonds out of where you are.

Research has shown realistic optimists make more of a difference in the world than pessimists. They also tend to be more successful. As Theodore Roosevelt said:

> It's not the critic who counts, not the man who points out how the strong man stumbled, or when the doer of deeds could have done better. The credit belongs to the man who is actually in the arena; whose face is marred by dust and sweat and blood; who strives valiantly; who errs and comes short again and again; who knows the great enthusiasms, the great devotions and spends himself in a worthy cause; who at the best, knows in the end the triumph of high achievement; and who at the worst if he fails, at least fails while daring greatly, so that his place shall never be with those cold and timid souls who know neither victory or defeat.[3]

Keep believing. Keep fighting. Keep dreaming.

Because when you do, your glass isn't just half full—it's overflowing.

God-Sized Dreamers Don't Do It All

I slumped in my chair at church. Looking around the room, I could see women who were feeding the hungry, raising kids, reaching out in our community, and leading Bible studies—just to name a few. I felt small and inadequate. I mentally began listing ways I could compensate: *If I volunteer at the shelter once a month, join another small group, up my goals. . . .* I quickly felt exhausted and thought perhaps God was simply fed up with me. Have you ever felt that way? I whispered a prayer for help.

About halfway through the message, our pastor pointed out into our very large congregation exactly to the place where I was sitting. "You are not the church," he said. "We are the church. You don't have to do it all." It was one of those moments when it seemed a heavenly spotlight shined on my soul, and I knew those words were for me. A smile broke out across my face, and the heaviness on my chest lifted again.

Our pastor went on to explain that we are each a part of the body of Christ and none of us can do everything. Instead we connect with each other and the Holy Spirit so we can all do exactly what we're called to. With all of us serving together, the needs get met.

If you are a God-sized dreamer, then you are saying no to some things in your life. They may be very good things. Even great things. But they are not for you. In our world today, saying yes can be so much easier than saying no. When we focus on what God has truly called us to do, we can face guilt, criticism, and misunderstanding. It's a brave choice.

Maybe no one has ever told you thank you for making those hard decisions. Thank you for not simply giving in and signing up or settling for someone else's agenda for your life. Thank you for keeping God first and listening to what he has called you to do. I know there are other voices. I know there are other opportunities. I know you could walk away. And you haven't. Good for you.

Good for us too. Because if you don't fulfill your role in the body of Christ, then no one else will. Sure, we may limp along and make it work, but it won't be the same. Like we've talked about before, you and what you contribute matter in an irreplaceable way.

God-sized dreamers don't do it all. They only do what God asks. I'm cheering you on in the yes you've said to what God has for your life. But I'm also cheering for the no you've had to say too. It's just as important and perhaps sometimes even more difficult.

Not doing it all means we can give our all to the One who matters most.

God-Sized Dreamers Feed Hungry Hearts

We carry slow cookers into the kitchen and set them on the table. Soup is ladled into bowls. Bread is neatly placed on plates. Dessert stands ready on a counter nearby. Outside hungry people wait. My community group is serving those in need tonight.

And aren't we all in need?

We wipe down the last of the surfaces a couple of hours later. I think of smiles as spoons are lifted to lips. I remember the laughter of children as they break off a piece of cookie. I recall the looks of satisfaction and fullness as folks lean back in their chairs when they're done.

Where have I seen all of that before?

I realize then that I see it every day. I see it when a co-worker pauses to offer a kind word to someone having a hard day—a little morsel of encouragement that's gobbled up with gratitude. I see it when my friend wraps her arms around her oh-so-tired little one and sees past the crankiness to the silent request for comfort and rest. I see it when a stranger on the street flashes a smile like an unexpected bit of chocolate tossed my way.

If I were with you now, I know I'd see it there too. You're feeding someone today. *Who is the hungry heart in your life?* Oh, what you do may feel small. It may feel unseen. But it matters. It's noticed by the one who said, "And if anyone gives even a cup of cold water to one of these little ones who is my disciple, truly I tell you, that person will certainly not lose their reward" (Matt. 10:42).

Just in case no one has told you lately, I want to whisper this: *Thank you for what you do. Thank you for feeding the hungry in your life in your own amazing way.*

We carry the Crock-Pots back to our cars. The fall wind feels like a whisper around us. Every last bit is gone. We didn't even get to eat, but I don't feel hungry. It turns out those whose bodies we fed did the same for our hearts in return.

And so it goes—round and round. Giving, receiving, in need, meeting needs too.

Until we're all so very full.

God-Sized Dreamers Pursue a Different Kind of Ambition

It's easy to get caught up in the comparison game. We live in a society that tells us bigger is better, more is more, and getting to the top is the ultimate achievement.

I know that kind of ambition.

She calls my name. She tells me I'm not enough yet.

She blurs my perspective so that I can't see the goodness right in front of me.

She tells me that I must try harder, work longer, go further than I am right now.

But then these words: "Make it your ambition to lead a quiet life," says the apostle Paul (1 Thess. 4:11).

What?

I don't know *this* ambition.

It sounds so much more like my Savior.

The One who calls me to smallness, to stillness, to peace and life.

The One who whispers, "You are enough in me because I am enough in you."

The One who stops me from striving, who gives me permission to slow down, who tells me my worth is already won forever.

Yes, this is the ambition I want to live with, to live *for*.

A quiet life . . . *especially on the inside.*

Where all the demands and lies have been silenced, and all that's left is ambitious, outrageous, scandalous Love calling my name.

God-sized dreamers know that we're not called to be the biggest and best. We're not called to strive. Yes, in the journey of our dream we may be called into the spotlight. We may find ourselves in a position of tremendous influence. But we don't ever have to pursue it.

Our role is obedience. God's role is results. So thank you for being faithful in the quiet and small, in the unnoticed and ordinary. What you do is a beautiful sacrifice. Your life that may feel so insignificant at times may be just right for the kingdom and have an impact far beyond what the world (and you) can see with your eyes.

God-Sized Dreamers Trust His Love

God surprised me the other night. Does he ever do that to you?

As lights in the sanctuary flickered low, we paused for a moment to pray. My pastor said, "Ask God to show you what you need to see in your heart."

I waited to hear a flaw, a struggle, a secret sin unknown even to me. But the words that drifted into my heart were the last ones I expected to hear.

"Stop doubting my love."

My head snapped up.

Stop doubting my love?

Could that be right?

Yet as I glanced at my husband sitting next to me, I knew it was true. The moments in our marriage that grieve him most deeply are when, for some reason or another, I find it hard to believe he really loves me. It's not about him—it's about me. Insecurities. Past wounds. Believing I have to be perfect.

I began to understand. After all, I'm the bride of Christ, say the sacred pages. Wouldn't doubting his love grieve him too?

I whispered a prayer of repentance of receiving the love that's already mine, of opening my heart more fully to the One who pursues me relentlessly. And you too.

You are loved.

More than you know.

More than you see.

More than you've even dared to dream.

We can stop doubting.

We can be secure in Love.

"And so we know and rely on the love God has for us" (1 John 4:16).

By the time the lights went back up in the sanctuary, I felt all lit up on the inside too.

Full of joy.

Fully loved.

God-sized dreamers know they don't have to work harder and strive more to earn God's love. Instead they rest in it. Draw life from it. Let it be the fuel for their dreams and all they do. You can risk as a dreamer because you are secure in God's love. Thank you for daring to believe that what he says, he really means. Faith is believing in God, but it's also believing—only because of Jesus—that he also believes in us.

God-Sized Dreamers Embrace Enough

I sometimes look in the mirror or at my life, see all I am, then say, "Not good enough."

You too?

And yet . . .

God saw all that he had made (that means people too), and then he said, "Very good" (see Gen. 1:31).

It seems scandalous to believe that's true. Yet who am I to argue with the One who spoke the stars into place, who spread the seas as far as we can see, who numbers every hair on my messy, imperfect head?

It's not because of who we are but Whose we are.

Not because of what we've done but what Love has done for us.

Not temporary but forever and ever because he doesn't change.

I'm going to try to stop saying "not good enough" and instead dare to agree with the Love that will not let me go.

Want to join me?

I believe that this is the heart, the foundation of God-sized dreams. Because the temptation is to make our dreams about proving that we are enough, and then they become about us. But when we begin from a place of love, belonging, and acceptance, our dreams are about the One who calls us. We can move forward from a place of inner peace no matter how busy our lives may be. We can trust that what we do is also enough because we understand our part is obedience.

Thank you for being a dreamer who doesn't always try to prove her worth. I get credit card applications all the time that declare, "Preapproved!" The same is true of you. God has already approved you for your God-sized dream. He has already given you all you need and made you all you need to be. He will make everything unfold in his way, his time. What you're doing today may not feel like enough. But if you're simply saying yes to Jesus and whatever he asks, then it is more than enough—it's world changing. And so are you.

Your Heart

Your most valuable asset as a God-sized dreamer isn't the plans you can make or the connections you have. It's not the talents you possess or the experiences you can list. It's your heart.

That's where the One who gives you dreams and makes them come true dwells. It's where you hear his voice and learn how to follow faithfully. It's where you love, which is the most beautiful dream of all.

Guard your heart like you would a priceless treasure. It's of great worth and can't be replaced by anyone or anything.

You are a gift to this world, my friend. We need more God-sized dreamers like you. Carry on with a smile on your face, joy in your steps, and your heart held high, because you belong to One who loves you more than you can even imagine.

Go Deeper Guide

(Download a printable version with lines for writing at www.holley gerth.com on the "Books & More" page.)

1. Describe a God-sized dreamer in your life. What stands out most about them to you?
2. Where does God have you right now? How can you be faithful where you are today so you're ready for where he wants to take you tomorrow?
3. What helps you keep your heart open to God, those around you, and the dreams he has for you?
4. Who are you encouraging? We all have a circle of influence in our lives (for example, family, friends, church). Who is in yours?
5. Would you describe yourself as naturally a "glass half full" or "glass half empty" type of person? What impacts your attitude most?
6. What hard no have you said in order to pursue a God-sized dream? Are there others you might need to say too?
7. "Make it your ambition to lead a quiet life" (1 Thess. 4:11). How do these words make you feel? If you described your ambition in words, what would you say? "My ambition is to . . ."

Dream It. Do It.

Draw your circle of influence and write in names as well as how each person is connected to your God-sized dream.

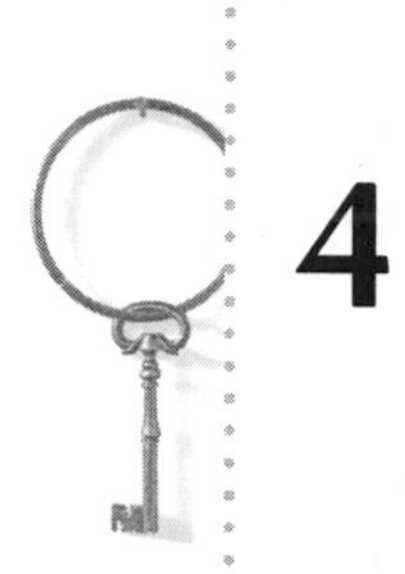

4

What Comes Next for You?

In the movie *While You Were Sleeping*, actress Sandra Bullock plays the role of Lucy—a single young woman who carries around a passport without any stamps. She sits in a toll booth dreaming of faraway places until falling in love changes that forever. As the movie goes along, Lucy begins to realize that dreaming isn't the same as doing. She eventually faces her fears, opens her heart, and discovers that there's more to life after all.

It's tempting to hide our dreams away. We tell ourselves we'll pursue them later or that we need to feel safer first. But the reality is, later may not come and living out a dream is risky no matter when we decide to do it. Like Lucy, we all have to come to a point when we're ready to stop simply dreaming and begin *doing*. In other words, "Faith without deeds is useless" (James 2:20).

Most dreams never see the light of day. But not yours. You are brave and determined. You are going to say yes to whatever it is God is asking you to do. I just know it.

Even when we decide to truly pursue our dreams, it's still challenging to know what to do next. We wonder, "What steps do I take?" The transition from blue-sky thinking to the solid, practical ground can be bumpy. But it can be done, and that's when the fun really gets started. It just takes time, intention, planning, and lots of prayer.

Defining Your Dream

At first we catch just a glimpse of our dream. It's vague and blurry. Perhaps a conversation draws our attention or a surprisingly compelling idea pops into our minds in the shower. Slowly that outline begins to fill with more color and detail. Over time we begin to see it, really see it.

It's tempting to charge ahead at this point. But now is the time to stop and study your dream carefully. One way to do that is to define your dream in one to three sentences.

Those sentences need three distinct parts. First, the "what" of your dream. This is exactly as it sounds—a description of what you want to accomplish. For example, "My dream is to transition out of my job and be a stay-at-home mom with my kids." Or you might say, "My dream is to get promoted to partner in my company."

It can feel scary to write this down. Up until now, your dream may have been something you liked to take out, hold, look at, and then tuck safely back within your heart. But now you're putting it out there. As you do this, a thousand reasons why this dream is ridiculous, you're not qualified, or the time isn't right will come rushing into your head. Ignore them. They're just a sign that you're on the right track—the resistance that we all encounter as we actually begin to take steps forward. Those words can't hurt you, and with Jesus you are far stronger than those lies.

Write the "what" of your dream here:

After you put your "what" in place, it's time to take a look at the "why" of your dream. God-sized dreams take too much time, effort, and passion to do them "just because it sounds like fun." This journey is going to take commitment, tenacity, and a stubborn willingness to be obedient no matter what happens. The "why" behind your dream is essential.

Start by writing down the first thing that comes to mind. You might say, "I want to be promoted to partner in my company because I can have more influence than ever before with my coworkers." Or you might say, "I want to be promoted to partner in my company because I'm competitive and I can't stand it that the woman who sits next to me might beat me to it." Whatever the reason, it's okay to admit it. God already knows.

Once you put your "why" out there, it's time to ask God if your agenda matches his. Is this a "why" that resonates with his heart too? Has he given you the reason behind this dream, or does it come from a place that might not be healthy or happy?

A little disclaimer: We are human, and having 100 percent pure motives is impossible for us. We will always struggle with our flesh as we pursue our dreams. There will always be a "little bit of me" mixed in as you move forward. If you wait to have all of that resolved, then you will never pursue your dream. What we're talking about here is your *primary* motivation, not your *only* motivation. Whenever you do anything, you will have a thousand different reasons behind it. Don't let that make you feel guilty or deter you. Just be honest about it, deal with any part of it that you need to, and keep moving forward anyway.

Write the "why" behind your dream here:

....

....

....

The "why" behind your dream should fit with who you are overall. In my book *You're Already Amazing*, we walked together through a process of creating a LIFE (Love Is Faith Expressed) statement. If you haven't done that already, I'd encourage you to do so. Even if it's not through the book, think about what your mission or purpose statement might look like. The simplest way to do so can be using this approach.

We all start with a common foundation based on Galatians 5:6:

I am created and called to express my faith through love . . .

Now you'll finish that statement with your unique way of doing so in the world. That part will have this structure:

. . . especially by (verb ending in "ing") + (what) + (who) + (how)

Here's my LIFE statement:

I am created and called to express my faith through love,

especially by bringing hope and encouragement
(*what*)

to the hearts of women through words.
(*who*) (*how*)

Another one might be:

I am created and called to express my faith through love,

especially by meeting the practical needs of
(*what*)

my family, friends, and community through service.
(*who*) (*how*)

Try yours here (this is just a start—you can think and pray about it more later):

I am created and called to express my faith through love, especially by

....

....

(verb ending in "ing") + (what) + (who) + (how)

The sentence structure above is just a suggestion. You can write your LIFE any way that you'd like. It can be shorter, longer, or in an entirely different format. *There is no wrong way to do this.*

Think of this statement as your umbrella. Everything you pursue in life should fit under it. Especially for those of us who are visionaries, what looks like a dream can actually turn out to be a distraction. We love what's new and shiny. It seems so appealing—surely that's what we should be doing! I remember my wise mentor in college, Beth English, used to say, "Holley, the hardest choices in life are not between bad and good. They are between good and best." You will have many opportunities and options in your life. You will even have many God-sized dreams. But I believe you will only have one primary purpose. Yes, you will live this out in very different ways throughout the varying seasons of your life. But at the heart, it will remain remarkably the same.

If your dream and your purpose don't align, then it's time to take a step back. One of three things could be happening. First, maybe the purpose you thought fit so well actually needs to be expanded. Sometimes dreams can shine a light on your soul in a new, deeper way. Or it may be that this dream is worthwhile, but it's not for you. It may be appealing for a variety of reasons—a new adventure, money, prestige, or the people you get to connect with along the way. But every yes is a no to one or more things too, and following this dream could lead you away from what you're truly called to do. Finally, it may be that God is asking you to take a specific detour from your primary purpose for a certain season.

You have a unique mission, and whatever God calls you to do will fit with that in some way. A line in a popular movie says, "I don't know where we're going, but we're making good time!" Before you move forward, make sure you're headed in the right direction.

Know Your Destination

As I just described, knowing your direction is important, but so is understanding the destination for your dreams. What is the end result you have in mind? What does it seem God is asking you to accomplish?

I have to admit this is tricky for me because I'm not much of a specific goal setter. The good news is, you don't always need a ten-point plan for everything you do. We are all wired differently. If you get a thrill from writing out detailed lists and checking them off, then go for it. But if you're more of a free spirit who needs wide boundaries, then that can work out well too. Corporate culture in particular can be very focused on goals that are attached to numbers. That can spill into our God-sized dreams too. We have to sell X books or have X profit. Again, if that kind of goal setting works well for you, great. But if it makes you want to hyperventilate, then just realize you don't have to pursue your dream in that way.

What you do need, however, is an idea of your ultimate destination. Imagine getting in a car and saying, "I'm just going to drive until I run out of gas." If what you want is a spontaneous, flexible experience, you'll probably be fine with wherever you end up. But if deep down you actually wanted to make it to the beach, you may be disappointed when you wind up in a fast-food restaurant parking lot in the middle of a rural highway.

It can seem presumptuous to decide on a destination. We pray, "Lord, I'll go wherever you want me to go." Then we sit in a car with the gear in neutral and our hands locked on the steering wheel, waiting for further instructions. A few times in Scripture, God speaks to people when they're in this position. *But most of the time he meets them along the way and redirects them.* Think about the apostle Paul on the road to Damascus. Moses in the desert with the burning bush. The disciples in the middle of their everyday work of being fishermen.

They were all doing *something*.

Then God stepped in and radically changed their course.

Most of us know the verse in Isaiah that says, "But they that wait upon the LORD shall renew their strength; they shall mount up with wings as eagles; they shall run, and not be weary; and they shall walk, and not faint" (40:31 KJV). What's interesting to me is that this Scripture has so many verbs. And it doesn't say sitting! Walking and running, yes, but staying in place isn't there.

Perhaps our idea of waiting is too limited. We think we have to be still and do nothing at all. But what if waiting is more about the attitude of our hearts? We move forward with a sense of expectation and are open at any moment to God redirecting us.

Yes, there are times to truly be still. For example, we often quote the verse, "Be still, and know that I am God" (Ps. 46:10). In looking at the context for that verse, it's in a time of war and great trouble. God is reassuring his people that he will defend them. Sometimes it's the same in our lives. But usually when we have a God-sized dream, it's a time for offense and not defense. Ask God specifically, "Do you want me to be completely still?" If not, then it's okay to start taking steps as long as you keep an open heart and open hands along the way.

It can also be intimidating to actually say, "Well, this is the outcome I'd like for my God-sized dream." As soon as we do, fear is there to start whispering, "But it might not work and then you'll look like a failure." The reality is, we don't know what will happen. Most likely what we decide as our destination won't turn out to be where we end up. *And that's okay.*

My youth pastor's wife once gave me a bookmark that said, "Shoot for the moon. If you miss, you'll still land on a star." Dream big. Write down crazy things. Go wild with your imagination. Bust down the wall of fear by thinking up something so impossible that it takes your fear by surprise and you slip right past it.

Say that thing you would never dare to admit out loud.

Know where you want to go.

Then lay it down. Surrender that goal to Jesus and tell him, "This is where I think you want me to go. So I'm moving forward.

Rush, rush.

Are there ever enough hours in the day?

It seems a voice whispers to my heart,

"Not for your agenda—but always for Mine."

I stop, sigh, smile.

The most important "done" in my life is not the one I hope to write on my list at the end of the day. Instead it's the one I hope to hear at the end of my life:

"Well done, good and faithful servant."

Ah, yes, I'm called to relationship, not accomplishment.

And I'm loved no matter how many items on my list are left unchecked.

Whew.

I'm so glad.

You too?

But you are Lord of my life, and you can change my path at any step along the way. What matters most to me is that I'm obedient to you."

Then go.

What's your destination? Where do you want to end up with your God-sized dream?

Figure Out How to Get to Your Destination

After you decide to move forward, it's time to map out where you're headed. Every kid knows there's only one question that matters when you're on a road trip: "Are we there yet?" Kids ask that question because they can't look out the window, see the sign for mile marker 108, and say, "Ah yes, we are 15.2 minutes from Grandma's house." When we don't know how to tell where we are along the way, we become frustrated. Planning in advance can help us avoid feeling lost and confused.

Sometimes God deliberately chooses to keep us guessing. We're not sure where he's taking us or what route we'll end up on along the way. But most of the time there's room for strategy when it comes to our God-sized dreams, and it's part of being a good steward.

Strategy can sound like a big, intimidating word, but really it just means "how we'll get from here to there." It's the mental equivalent of pulling out a map and charting your course from one point to another. Sure, there may be road construction and you get rerouted. Or perhaps you go out of your way to check out the quaint little restaurant in the middle of town. But overall, you know which roads are likely to lead you to your desired destination.

A little heads-up: creating a strategy can cause fear at first because it feels like there has to be *one right way*. But there isn't. Any destination has multiple paths to arrive at it. Some might take a little longer or be a bit more complex, but eventually you get there. Sometimes we delay starting at all because we're just not sure that we've found the perfect path. But the most important part is simply moving forward.

When you look for guidance, you'll quickly discover there are tons of books on how to think strategically. Most involve complicated systems, project maps, and long lists. Can I make a confession? Those things make me want to hide under a table.

My approach to strategic planning? I use an unlined journal and draw shapes with lots of lines connecting one thing to another. Then I transfer any specific tasks to my calendar. Done.

About every month or so, I draw a new version of what's going on and make updates as needed based on what's happened. Often my strategy looks like this:

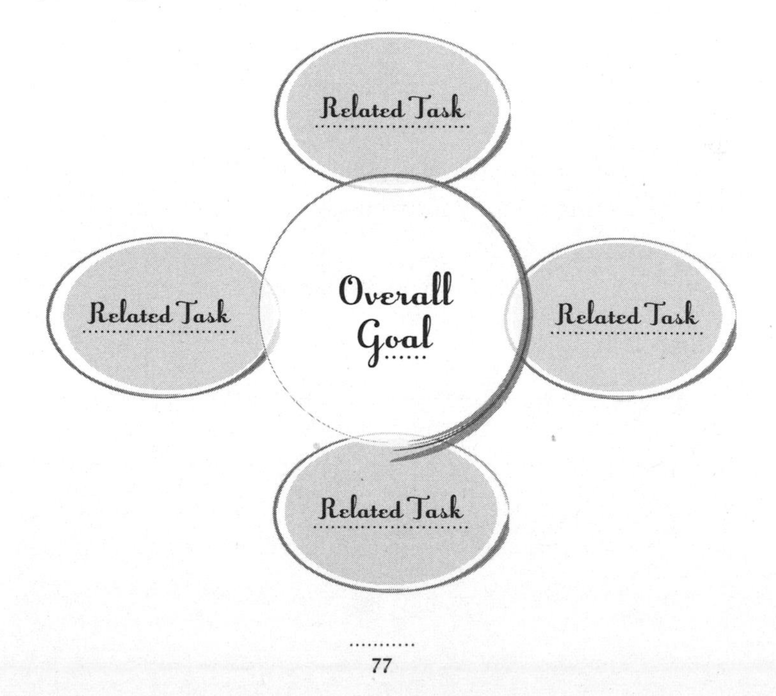

Long lists stress me out. Intricate systems distract me. Maintaining things feels boring to me. Yet I'm productive and most often reach my goals. I even scored very high on "Strategic" in the test from the book *Now, Discover Your Strengths*.[4]

I say all that simply to dismiss the myth that there is one right way to do goal setting and strategic thinking. The best strategy is one you'll actually do because it fits with who you are.

Think about how God wired you. Are you an outgoing, social person? Then having other people highly involved in your God-sized dream along the way should probably be part of your strategy. Are you motivated by details? Then you might want to get one of those very specific books on strategy and map out your plan. It is up to you and the Holy Spirit to decide how to best pursue your God-sized dream.

I do believe having some kind of strategy in place, however formal or informal it may be, is important because it will make you intentional. Life is busy. Other priorities pop up. We're all vulnerable to the urgent overshadowing what's truly important. Strategy makes you focus and also lets you know if you're making progress.

If you need a starting place, you can use the template below as a basic beginning for your strategy.

My God-Sized Dream

- **Step One**

  What I will do: ______________________________

  When I will do it: ______________________________

  How I will know it's done: ______________________________

  ____

- **Step Two**

  What I will do: ______________________________

  When I will do it: ______________________________

  How I will know it's done: ______________________________

  ____

- **Step Three**

  What I will do: ______________________________

  When I will do it: ______________________________

  How I will know it's done: ______________________________

  ____

You can add as many steps as you need. You might feel a bit of panic looking at this section, because this is where the rubber meets the road. This is where the dream starts making the transition from your heart into the world. And that, my friend, is always scary. You will feel resistance when you get serious about putting your dream on paper. You will begin to think that it's not the right time, there's more you need to research, or maybe you're not prepared. *Do it anyway.*

Like we talked about before, God can and will reroute you if needed. And most likely the steps you write above as well as the destination will change. That's okay. What you're looking for here is momentum and progress. Have you ever tried to steer a parked car? It's a tough proposition. Just get in gear and start heading down the road. The rest will work itself out as you go.

Know What You Need to Take with You

After you've scoped out a destination and plotted your course along the way, you'll have an idea of what to pack for the journey. Swimsuit? Parka? Raincoat? Every God-sized dream is different, and it's important to be prepared.

Some people might say, "Well, God will just provide what I need along the way." Yes, that's true. But I also believe he gives us wisdom to know how to plan and prepare as well. Knowing what you may encounter along the way helps you get ready before you find yourself in a tough situation that could have been avoided.

For example, you may know that starting a blog is going to be part of reaching your God-sized dream. If so, then it's time to do some research about what technology you need. If you know you'll require child care for a few hours a week, then it's time to start asking friends about who they recommend. If your dream involves something physical, then it's time to get off the couch and go for a walk each evening.

What do you *not* have right now that you will need along the way?

Look ahead and ask yourself that question. Then go about getting it. Sure, that doesn't seem super-spiritual. But Scripture is also full of really practical advice, especially in Proverbs. The world is set up to work in certain ways, and when we ignore that and go running ahead without wisdom, we shouldn't be surprised at the consequences.

Here's the reality: *God-sized dreams are a lot of work*. It can seem like because we have this grand vision, it will all just fall into place. But that never happens. Ever. You have to be prepared to do the work. Over and over again.

You "reap what you sow," and in order to get a lot out of a God-sized dream, you'll have to put a lot into it. There's just no way around that truth. Yes, God is the one who makes the results happen, but we are clearly called to put in effort. This isn't "works" in the sense that we are trying to earn God's approval by what we do. Nor is it "striving" where we feel the burden is on us to make everything happen. It's simply good, honest, hard work to pursue what God has put in front of us with excellence.

Be prepared. Work hard. Persevere. God-sized dreams are many things, but "easy" is not one of them.

Don't Quit, No Matter What

At some point in pursuing your dream, you will get tired. You will sit down on the side of the road and say, "For crying out loud, if I knew it was going to be this hard and take this long, I never would have started down this path."

Your job in those moments is simply this: don't quit.

Because just over the next hill, just around the next bend is the breakthrough you've been waiting for, and you will miss it if you stop now.

I've pursued enough God-sized dreams to know that's almost always the case. Just when you feel like you're done, just when you think you can't go on, that's when the door opens and unexpectedly you're there.

When we think that there's only one path to our God-sized dreams and it doesn't work out, then we can assume that we have to go back and start over. But that's not true. Just find another way. It doesn't mean you've done anything wrong. It doesn't mean you messed up. It simply means that we live in a fallen world and there will always be obstacles and detours.

The key is to not keep beating your head against the same roadblock. As quickly as you can, pull out your strategy and rewrite it. Don't feel guilty, beat yourself up, or get mad at whoever put that roadblock there in the first place. Just say, "Well, I found one more way that didn't work. That means I'm closer to finding a path that does get me there. I learned some things on that detour, and I'll be wiser as I move ahead. Now I'm going to get back at it again."

We all know the saying that goes, "Where there's a will, there's a way." I'd revise that just a bit to say, "Where there's *God's will*, there's a way." As much as it may seem like we're up against the impossible, there's nothing God can't do. Anything is possible with him. That means if this God-sized dream is truly one he's planted in your heart, he will make it happen *no matter what*. Your God-sized dream is invincible in his hands.

What's most likely to defeat you isn't external circumstances or challenges, it's *you*. Don't give in to discouragement, doubt, or fear. Don't let the enemy tell you that you've goofed this up for good and it's over. Just keep going.

You will get there, one way or another.

Keep Your Dream in Front of You

Most God-sized dreams aren't discarded; they're simply overcome by distractions. The pile of laundry stares us in the face while our dream waits quietly in a corner. A stack of bills that needs to be paid demands our attention while our goal of writing a book silently sits somewhere on our hard drive. In one way God-sized dreams can be very loud, but in another way they don't ever demand to be heard. If you push them away or quiet them down, eventually they'll comply.

It's your job to give your dream a presence and voice in your life. Keep it in front of you. That might mean hanging a reminder on your fridge, making a task list on your computer, writing notes on your calendar, or even having a friend call you once a week to ask how it's going. Whatever you need to do, keep your dream and strategy in front of you.

Be aware of what pulls you away from your dream. How do you procrastinate? What do you choose instead? What are the "When I . . ." statements that place your dream somewhere in the future rather than right here, right now?

Because God-sized dreams feel so powerful, we often take it for granted that they will happen someday. But that's not true. In several studies, older people were asked what they regretted most. The answer? Not what they did but *what they didn't do.*

No matter how passionately you feel about your dream, that is not enough to make it a reality. There have to be actions attached to your emotions. Talking about your dream doesn't count either. Yes, that's an important part of the process. But at some point you've got to shift from your lips to your hands and just do the work. Don't be fooled into believing that saying something is the same as getting it done.

You will have to fight for your dream. There will never be the "right" time. There will never be the "perfect opportunity." There will never be the "easy way." If your dream is going to come into being, it's going to take a lot of hard work, perseverance, and leaps of faith with Jesus that you never thought you could complete.

But you will.

I know it.

I feel it.

You are going to make this happen. You're not going to quit. You're going to keep that dream in front of you and keep the One who gave it to you right beside you all the way.

Remember and Celebrate

The funny thing about dreams is how much they shift our focus to the finish line. But it turns out that the most satisfying part of a dream is often the journey along the way. Author Gretchen Rubin expresses it this way: "'Happiness,' wrote Yeats, 'is neither virtue nor pleasure nor this thing nor that, but simply growth. We are happy when we are growing.' Contemporary researchers make the same argument: that it isn't goal attainment but the striving after goals—that is, growth—that brings happiness."[5] It turns out that the completion of our dream is simply the cherry on top. But most of the goodness, most of the growth, happens long before what we desire ever becomes a reality, because along the way to our dream, we intimately experience God's presence in a powerful way. We're created to know and pursue him. In doing so, we find joy, meaning, and purpose.

So make time to celebrate along the way. Rejoice in each step completed. Take time to notice what is happening. Share those moments with those you love—and the God who loves you.

In the Old Testament, God often had the people of Israel stop and set up physical markers to remind them of what he had done in their lives. As humans, we're all tempted to just "move on to the next thing." But it's important to stop and reflect on how far we've come and how much God has done on our behalf.

Yes, we're to work hard, plan, and move forward diligently—but not to the extent that we become driven by our dream. I know what that's like. I also clearly remember a moment when it seemed God whispered to my heart, "If you're driven, you can't be led."

It's a fine line that we walk. We take responsibility for what God has entrusted to us, and yet in the end it's ultimately simply about obedience, about taking the next step of faith. The most important thing you can do for your dream? Pray, pray, and pray some more.

Pray words of praise when things go well.

Pray for wisdom when you're not sure which way to go.

Pray with thanks when God comes through beyond all you could have imagined.

Pray that in all you do, his purposes will prevail.

Even if you don't build an actual physical reminder of what God has done, let prayer be like stones you place in the path along the way to remind you of where you've been, where you're going, and who is walking with you.

Conclusion

You've done a lot of hard work in these last few pages. You've dared to define your dream and even to take steps to achieve it. Your heart may be pounding and your head spinning, but you are on your way. Your dream is no longer just an idea or a quiet whisper in your heart. It's becoming reality.

You can do this, my friend.

Keep going.

Keep believing.

Keep pursuing the God who never stops pursuing you.

Go Deeper Guide

(Download a printable version with lines for writing at www.holley gerth.com on the "Books & More" page.)

1. Finish this sentence: My God-sized dream is to . . .
2. Why do you want to pursue that God-sized dream?
3. What's your LIFE statement?
4. What do you specifically want to accomplish through this God-sized dream?
5. "Many are the plans in a person's heart, but it is the LORD's purpose that prevails" (Prov. 19:21). What are three goals and/or next steps that will help you move forward with this dream?
6. What do you not have right now that you will need along the way to your dream?
7. How will you celebrate as you take steps forward?

Dream It. Do It.

Create a one-page strategy for your dream. Include what your God-sized dream is, what you specifically want to accomplish, and the steps you'll take as well as a due date for each one. Keep this strategy in a place where you can clearly see it. It's not set in stone and God can change it at any time, but having it in front of you will help you stay focused.

5

A Guide to Overcoming **Your Fear**

Here's a little secret: it's not the work that's the hardest part.

Oh, we tell ourselves that's true—that the most difficult part of the dream will be writing the book, launching the business, making the decision. But it's one four-letter word that turns out to be the biggest foe of our dreams, the enemy of the "more" we long for in our lives.

Fear.

It growls at us in the dark. It whispers to us in the daylight. It tries to tell us that this is too much or we're not enough.

Fear is a bully who doesn't fight fair.

But like most bullies, fear doesn't stand its ground when you decide to turn and face it. And you can, my friend, *you can*. Let's talk about how to do that together.

Calling Fear's Bluff

She sends a note over email. "I'm stuck," she says. "I keep trying to take the next step, but every time I do I feel so much fear."

I softly smile when I read her words. She doesn't know it yet, but this is a *good* thing.

I place my fingers on the keyboard and type, "Fear camps out right next to whatever it is you're most called to do. That means the closer you get to your calling, the louder fear sounds. You must be headed in the right direction. Keep going—fear is a Chihuahua that sounds like a Doberman."

A few days later she wrote back that she'd pushed past the fear, and yes, when she looked fear in the face, it wasn't at all the intimidating beast it appeared to be from a distance.

You will face fear. Fear is a response to a threat. It means there's risk and something you value is on the line. If you don't feel that way about your dream, then it's not close enough to God's calling for you.

So why do we resist fear so much? There are many reasons, but one of the primary ones is a myth that holds many of us back: *fear is a sin.*

I've heard that my whole life. So for a long time I sidestepped anything that caused me to feel fear because I assumed it must not be God's will. But as I dug deeper into Scripture, it became clear that fear itself isn't a sin any more than other emotions we have, such as happiness, anger, or grief. All emotions are just messages about what we're experiencing. Imagine if you couldn't feel fear. You'd be vulnerable in a lot of ways. The initial fear response is a gift from God that tells us, "Hey, be alert and pay attention to this," or perhaps even, "Do something!"

God wired our minds in beautiful ways. Fear comes from our amygdala, the area of our brain that controls the "flight or fight" response. When we feel fear, our body releases chemicals that direct us to do one of those two things—either get out of the situation or get ready for a rumble. In our modern world, that "flight or fight" isn't often triggered by actual physical threats like a lion on the side of the road. Instead it's more often set off by the lion described as the enemy of our souls (see 1 Pet. 5:8), waiting to pounce on our hearts when we're hot on the trail of God-sized dreams.

When we feel fear, God understands, because he's the one who made us that way. In many ways, that first response is involuntary. He designed our minds that way so we could react quickly in dangerous situations without being slowed down by the rational thought process, which takes much longer.

Surprise: fear is not a sin—it's a gift.

All throughout Scripture God does talk to his people about fear. As I dug into those verses, two primary phrases appeared. God says, "Do not fear" or "Do not be afraid" almost one hundred times. That may make it seem like fear is a sin. But if you look closely, those phrases are almost always in contexts where the audience God is addressing is *already* feeling fear.

"Do not be afraid" appears more than any other place in the story of the Israelites going to the Promised Land. God says, "Do not be afraid," and then he gives instructions about what to do next—commands, like going into battle, that he knows will cause even more fear to spring up. In essence, he's telling his people, like a father would tell his kids when they're scared in the dark or about to jump off the high dive for the first time, "Don't be afraid. Go ahead and jump. It will be okay."

I love that the word *be* is in that phrase. God doesn't say, "Don't feel fear." Because he made us, he understands that would be impossible. Instead he says, "Don't *be* afraid." In other words, don't *live* in fear or make it part of your identity.

You will feel fear. More than once. But you don't have to live in fear. You don't have to make that Chihuahua your pet and carry it around in your bag like a socialite. You don't have to pet it, give it treats, and let it sleep in your bed at night.

I mentioned before that fear is a response from the area of our brains called the amygdala that bypasses our rational thought. But after that first surge, the other parts of our brain do kick in, and that's when we have a decision to make.

Our amygdala says, "Ack! A threat! Fear alert!"

Then the rest of our brain starts searching for evidence to support or disprove that initial response. Is the monster we thought we saw in our closet actually the vacuum cleaner? Is the loud noise that sounded like a gunshot actually just a car backfiring?

With examples like those above, it's easy to shoo away the fear with physical evidence. But when it comes to the heart, it becomes much harder. Because most of the time there isn't a black-and-white answer to that fear. We have to respond by faith.

One of my pastors, Matt Newman, likes to say, "When David saw how big Goliath was, he could say either, 'He's too big for me to ever win' or 'He's too big for me to miss—and my God is even bigger.' "

Pick the first option and fear takes over, David runs for the hills, and history changes forever. Pick the second and you get a boy with a slingshot who chooses to stand boldly in faith and goes on to become the most well-known king of Israel.

This is the place where we get to choose obedience or rebellion. It's a myth that all fear is sin, but it's quite true that *fear can lead us into sin*. We can say no to what God asks of us. We can listen to the lies more than the truth. We can compromise our calling.

Most of us already know that's true. So we say, "Hey, fear might get me in trouble. So I'll avoid anything that makes me afraid." But saying that is a bit like saying, "Hey, water is kind of dangerous—I could drown—so I'll just never go near any kind of water." A better solution? Learn to swim.

The same is true of fear. And unlike avoiding water, which you possibly could do, getting around situations that make you feel afraid is impossible in this life. The cost of doing so is also much too high. If you decide never to feel fear, then in essence you are saying you will not complete God's purpose for your life, because doing so always involves fear in some way.

The first step to overcoming fear is to stop avoiding it. If avoidance is your only plan, the Chihuahua of fear will chase you down the street and nip at your heels forever. You will spend all your time and energy trying to escape fear when you could be using it to pursue your dreams instead. Stop and face the fear. Say, "Yes, I'm afraid. But fear isn't going to kill me. It's not even going to maim me. Fear has no power in my life. It's all bark and no bite. I'm going to move forward in faith. Fear may come my way, but I am not going to let it control me."

Facing your fear also lets you get a good look at it. Because we tend to avoid it, we often don't even know much about our fear. Where did it come from? What's it really saying to us? We've been talking about fear like it's a single Chihuahua. But really there's a whole herd. There might be the one wearing the pink collar that's the mean girls from high school yapping, "You're never going to fit in," or the one wearing the cute little sweater your grandma knitted barking, "That dream of yours just isn't practical."

Pause and write down your fears. Picture in your mind a Chihuahua for each one and name it. (Yes, I realize this is pretty ridiculous—but sometimes making your fear look silly is just what's needed. How many times has it threatened to make *you* look silly? Well, it's time to turn the tables. Take that, fear.)

My fears:

....

....

....

After you've written down your fears, look closely at them. Denise Martin, my life coach, went through a similar process with me when fears seemed especially loud in my life. After I wrote out my fears, she asked me questions about each one until eventually I realized the fears that seemed so real to me now were actually just echoes of lies from years ago.

So what do you do with that herd of Chihuahuas? You probably want to donate them to the local animal shelter. But it doesn't work that way. Each one of those fears is attached to something important in your life. To completely get rid of the fear would mean letting the other part (like a dream) go too. Your Chihuahuas are here to stay. You might decide you'll just swat them with a newspaper every time they nip at your heels. So whenever you feel fear, you spout out a cliché or slap a quick verse on the situation. But that's exhausting and ultimately not very effective.

Those puppies need to go to obedience school. Because here's the thing—fear always thinks it's the master. Sometimes it convinces you of the same. But it's not true.

You are the boss of fear and God is the boss of you.

That fear has got to learn to sit and submit.

Sure, it may still bark when someone rings the doorbell (that initial brain response we talked about). But you can teach it to behave nicely when you open the door.

Is this hard to do? Yep, especially at first. But over time fear learns who holds the leash, and while those fears may still be in your yard, they will no longer be wreaking havoc on your life and dreams.

How to Train Your Fear

You may have heard of Cesar Millan, the "dog whisperer" with an uncanny ability to alter the behavior of pups. I'd like to step in and be your own personal "fear whisperer" for the next few pages. I'm thinking that would look pretty awesome on a business card or T-shirt. Yes, ma'am.

Here are a few little things I've learned about fear.

Fear Responds to Truth, Not Commands

When we're not busy running from it, we like to boss our fear around. We throw commands at it. We tell it to go away, sit, fetch, or whatever else might make it settle down and let us get back to business.

But fear is a rebellious beast. It doesn't listen to commands *at all*. In fact, it's more likely to turn around and bite you on the toe than do what you say.

However, fear does respond to truth. When God is speaking to his people about fear, he often follows the directive not to be afraid with a promise about who he is and what he will do. For example, "Do not fear, for I am with you; do not be dismayed, for I am your God. I will strengthen you and help you; I will uphold you with my righteous right hand" (Isa. 41:10). We can grab hold of these truths and repeat them when fear comes at us. David does just that when he says, "The LORD is with me; I will not be afraid" (Ps. 118:6). He goes on to finish the psalm by listing what God has done for him.

Like we talked about, our rational minds need evidence to know how to proceed once the initial fear response has passed. David is giving his heart and mind evidence so that fear backs down. If he said, "Go away, fear!" then nothing would happen. But when we speak truth, fear responds and settles down. This usually doesn't happen on the first try. Because fear causes our minds to respond automatically, really pushing past fear means building another automatic response that comes after the initial fear. That means creating a habit. You are training your fear—not just forcing it to obey in the moment. That takes time, patience, and lots of practice.

Fear Is Lazy

My husband and I often go for walks through our neighborhood in the evening. On the corner of our street, there's a pint-sized dog that has learned to squeeze through the fence so it can run after unsuspecting pedestrians. The first few times it happened, I jumped and started to run—which, as you might guess, only made that little dog chase me. My husband, on the other hand, simply kept walking calmly. That turned out to be the right approach, because before long the dog got bored and tired, so it slipped back under the fence to take a nap.

Fear is much the same way. When it comes after you, it seems like it has a ton of energy. It's barking, bouncing, bristling the fur on its back. But it doesn't have any stamina. Sure, if you run from it, then it has motivation to chase you. Walk calmly, steadily, in the direction you're called to go instead, and fear will opt for lying down in the grass almost every time.

Speak truth to fear as a start. If it listens, great. If it doesn't, then just ignore it and carry on with whatever God has told you to do.

Fear Needs a Leash

Sometimes fear is persistent and keeps walking beside you. In those cases, it's time to put that fear on a leash and remind it who's boss. I love the story of Queen Esther (see Esther 4). She has the opportunity to go before the king on behalf of her people. But she also knows that doing so uninvited could lead to her death. She's afraid, but in the end she says, "If I perish, I perish." Then she keeps walking forward in faith.

I can almost guarantee that as she stepped before the king and waited to see if she would be accepted or executed, her heart was pounding. Big dream. Big risk. There's no way she could have done that without anxiety.

If you can't get fear to obey or go away, then put it on a leash and bring it with you. Just remember that you are in control—not fear.

Fear Gets Bigger When You Feed It

Fear has enough food to survive on just by living in this world. But sometimes we fatten it up even more by giving it treats. Every time we believe a lie, it's like throwing a bone to fear. We indulge it with insecurity or offer it a bit more of our attention to nibble on. Fear eats it all up, and then we're surprised when it grows.

Sharon Wooten, who blogs at *Hiking Toward Home*, says:

> I have a fear, I know in the depths of my heart, I really need to get over.
>
> Fear of failure.
>
> Fear that it will be more messy than beautiful.
>
> But can't the messy be beautiful too?
>
> It is to God. Isn't it?
>
> Because if not for the messy there would be no need for grace.[6]

By changing her perspective, Sharon is learning to nourish her creativity instead of nurturing her fears.

An old story goes that a little girl asked her grandfather which dog would win if they happened to get into a fight. The grandfather replied, "The one you feed the most."

Don't feed your fear. Feed your faith.

Fear Has a Muzzle

Our town has a farmers' market on Saturdays. As we stroll through it, we see an abundance of all shapes and sizes of dogs with their owners. A few of the more ferocious-looking ones usually have muzzles. They may let out a bark that startles those standing nearby, but they can't do any real damage.

Fear is the same way. In the end, it can't directly harm you. The way fear causes damage in our lives is indirect. It scares us away from the door God wants us to knock on that day. It convinces us that we're not as strong or brave as God tells us we are. It chases us in the opposite direction of the dream we're called to pursue.

You can tell fear that the jig is up and it can bark as much as it wants, but you know it can't really get to you. If you don't let fear control you, then there's nothing it can do to hurt you.

It's time to take your fear to obedience school, my friend. Show it who's the master—and who's the Master of you.

Make Fear Work for You

If you've ever felt a surge of panic and slammed on the brakes just before you hit the car in front of you, then you know that fear can be your friend. Like I talked about earlier, fear is an emotion and emotions are neutral. They're not good or bad—they're just a way our brains relay messages to our bodies about what's going on in our world.

Now that you've trained your fear, you can go one step further and actually make it work for you. That's especially true when you're pursuing a God-sized dream. You may not like having fear around, but it actually has an important role to play as you take steps of faith.

Let Fear Warn You about Risks

When fear starts barking, it usually means there's a perceived risk around. It might turn out to be the neighbor's cat, or it could be a burglar in the backyard. Stop and listen to your fear. What is it directing you to pay attention to? Look closely and then decide if the threat is valid or not. For example, if fear says, "You don't have what it takes and you're going to fail," then respond with the truth that God has given you "everything you need for life and godliness" (see 2 Pet. 1:3). If fear says, "You haven't prepared at all for this speech, so you may not do as well as you could," then that's a legitimate warning and it's time to go practice a bit more.

How do you tell if fear is giving you a false alarm or if you really should pay attention? Helpful fear is about something specific that you can take action to correct. For example, you might be afraid to start a blog because you don't know much about the internet. But you can do some research and quiet that fear down. Harmful fear is general, often about your character, and is usually not something you can control. For example, "No one is going to like you at that conference" is sure to evoke fear, but it's not based in reality. In those cases, it's time to speak truth and then press on in spite of the fear.

Let Fear Tell You What's Important to You

Like I mentioned at the beginning of this chapter, if you don't feel any fear about something, then it's probably not a true area of passion in your life. Think of your biggest fears. They most likely involve what matters most to you. Your family. Your friends. Your calling. When it feels like there's a risk, ask yourself, "What am I afraid of losing?" If the answer is, "I might look foolish and lose a little of my pristine reputation if I don't do this speech perfectly," then it's probably worth making the leap. If the answer is, "If I take this new job and have to work eighty hours a week, it could destroy my marriage," that's a whole different story.

Whatever you value most will cause the most fear in your life. What does that mean? When we're making decisions about risks and we understand that fear points to what matters most, then we can make a plan to protect those things while still moving forward. For example, if you know God is calling you to take that job that may end up with eighty hours of work a week, then a serious conversation about boundaries with your potential boss might be in order. Let fear show you how to proactively guard what's sacred in your life, but don't let it paralyze you into inaction because there's a possibility of loss.

Life is risk. There are no guarantees. We also need to ask ourselves, "What might I lose if I *don't* do this?" Usually those answers are more subtle but just as essential. Inaction doesn't equal safety. Doing nothing is much more of a risk than doing the something God has commanded.

Be bold. Step out. But let fear add wisdom to your journey as you go.

Let Fear Energize You

Imagine you're a teenager at an amusement park. You hop on a roller coaster, pull down the safety bar, and begin the slow *click-click-click* to the top. With each passing second the fear grows, but so does the excitement. Your stomach drops at the first hill, but then you put your hands in the air and enjoy the ride. When you get off you exclaim breathlessly, "Let's do that again!"

Physically and chemically, fear resembles another emotion we experience—excitement. Both emotions put our bodies on high alert, make us focused, and get us ready for action. If fear were only negative, then roller coasters, scary movies, and haunted houses would quickly cease to exist. I'm not advocating that you go out and try those activities. I'm simply saying that when we feel in control of fear, it can actually be (dare I say it) *fun*.

Think of a moment when you took an intentional, well-planned, God-ordained risk. Maybe you spoke to a group of people. Perhaps you carried your first baby home from the hospital. Or you accepted a new role at work that stretched you out of your comfort zone. Oh, sure, there was fear. But there were also glorious emotions like anticipation, joy, and the feeling of being fully alive. Believe it or not, you have fear to thank for part of that.

So when you begin to feel your stomach tighten, pretend you're on that roller coaster and embrace the journey. Whee! Then do it again. And again.

Let Fear Lead You to Love

When the little dog in our neighborhood that I mentioned earlier comes racing toward us, I'm not as afraid as before, but I still instinctively reach for my husband's hand. I want to know that I'm safe and secure, that someone bigger and stronger than I am is ready and willing to fight on my behalf. I need to know that love is there and that it will win.

It's the same for our hearts. While our fears show up in various forms, ultimately they all point back to the deepest fear of all: that we won't be loved.

I might fail . . . and I won't be loved.

I could let everyone down . . . and I won't be loved.

I may step out and find myself alone . . . and I won't be loved.

When it comes to that deep fear, there's only one solution. Perfect love. And there's only One who offers it to our hearts. "There is no fear in love. But perfect love drives out fear, because fear has to do with punishment. The one who fears is not made perfect in love" (1 John 4:18). God says that he will take care of the fear in our lives. This isn't a one-time event. He sends that fear out through the doggy door, and the next day it may come sneaking back in. But he promises us that fear will not win. When we get to heaven and stand before him, because of the blood of his Son and his sacrifice on the cross, we will not be afraid. In the most important moment of our lives and the first step into eternity, fear will be completely gone.

Until then, love chases away fear as often as we ask. Think of the moments when you feel the most loved and accepted. Those are probably also the ones when you feel the least fear. When fear comes at you, ask God to hide you in his love, to draw you deeper into it, to whisper to your heart the truth you need to hear so that his voice is louder than anything else.

The more we grow in love, the more fear shrinks. That process will continue until we're safe forever in heaven.

Let Fear Expand Your Faith

Every time we choose to listen to love more than fear, our faith grows. We learn to trust more, to see God act in new ways in our lives, to let him take us places beyond where we could have dared to go before.

The sound of fear can also be an invitation. It can be a signal that God is asking you to go somewhere new with him, to get outside your comfort zone, to be part of an adventure.

As the Israelites approached the Promised Land, twelve scouts were sent to bring back a report (see Num. 13). Ten returned with fear nipping at their heels and influencing their words. Two returned with proclamations of faith. Joshua and Caleb saw the land

We all have times when fear growls at our door,
when doubt creeps in, when we feel so very small.
But those are the moments when God's love can be the biggest,
when he's there with open arms, with truth that reminds us
who we are.

And who are you?

- You are loved. (Ps. 103:11)
- You have a purpose. (Phil. 1:6)
- You are not alone. (Ps. 73:23)
- And you are stronger than you know. (Phil. 4:13)

Nothing can change that—
not this day, that situation, those thoughts inside your mind.
Who you are is secure in the hands of the One who made you,
the same One who spoke stars into being,
whose hands can stretch from one end of the sea to the other,
who counts every hair on your head.

Keep going, my sister.
Press in, press on, and never give up.
We will do this together.
With each other.
With him.

For as long as it takes.

as one with obstacles, yes, but even greater opportunities. We want it to be one or the other. But there's never a time when what God asks us to do feels completely safe. If we wait for the giants to move out on their own, the roads we need to appear, and the opposition to disperse, then we'll never take possession of what God has given us.

Faith without risk isn't faith. It's just facts.

If we want a nice, safe reality where we don't ever feel fear, then we're going to miss out on much of what God has for us.

God is not committed to your safety. He is committed to his kingdom and your ultimate good.

He promises you security, yes, but not a free-from-fear life.

And even if you were perfect, that would still be true.

Jesus was perfect, and God's plans for him still included a cross.

This life is short. You get one shot to fulfill your purpose. There's not a plan B for you.

God's plans for you are good, my friend. Not always safe. Hardly ever predictable. Far from what you imagined. But they are good because he is.

Let fear push you into faith . . . and into the everlasting arms waiting for you that promise to never let you go.

From Now On

You've looked fear in the face. You've seen it for what it is. Now all that remains is to choose what you will do.

In *The Dream Giver*, Bruce Wilkinson says, "My life changed the day I decided to never again run away from my Comfort Zone fears. When you think about it, stepping through fear is a small price to pay for a Big Dream. That one step—that we face many times in our lives—must be the universal price tag God had in mind. I think God wants to know whether we really want the wonderful gift of his Dream in our life."[7]

Over and over the phrase "Do not be afraid" is paired with another one in the Bible.

Be strong and courageous.

God doesn't ever command what's impossible.

So no matter how you feel, no matter how big the obstacles may seem, no matter how loud the fear may sound right now—you can move forward in faith.

And I know you will.

Because you are a brave daughter of the King, chosen and cherished by him. You are an Esther for this generation, and this is your "for such a time as this" (Esther 4:14).

Take that step. Make that move. Seize this moment.

We need you to complete your calling.

You and Jesus are stronger than the fear.

Together you're unstoppable.

So go for it, girl, and know that I'm cheering you on in my heart every step of the way as you do.

Lord,

I thank you for the one reading these words right now. You know the fears in her heart and how she longs to step out in faith even more. I pray you will take her by the hand, silence those fears, and lead her into all you have for her.

Thank you for the gifts that you have placed within her.

Thank you for the strength she has through you.

Thank you for the ways she is called to make a difference.

You are greater than our fears. Whatever you have asked us to do is possible with you because you are unstoppable. And when we are obedient, we are unstoppable in your plans for us too.

Please take us on a new adventure with you.

Amen.

Go Deeper Guide

(Download a printable version with lines for writing at www.holley gerth.com on the "Books & More" page.)

1. What are your biggest fears when it comes to your God-sized dreams?
2. What is the truth that tames each of those fears?
3. What risks could those fears be pointing out to you? What can you do about them?
4. What do those fears tell you about what's important to you?
5. How does "perfect love drive out fear" (see 1 John 4:18)?
6. How can these fears expand your faith?
7. Describe a time when you felt fear and pushed through anyway. What happened?

Dream It. Do It.

Confront one small fear this week. Maybe you've been putting off a phone call, avoiding a difficult task, or something else. Face that fear head-on, ask for God's help, and get it done. Then celebrate when you do.

6

The **Disclaimers**

I sat on the couch, legs curled up under me. It had been one of *those* days. My husband walked by and asked, "What's the matter?"

I responded, "I don't like my dream today. It's not how I pictured it. Right now it just feels like a bunch of hard work."

He shrugged and said, "All dreams are that way."

As I sat there and considered his words, I thought back over the different God-sized dreams in my life. And I realized there had always been moments like this one along the way. Always.

I remember how before I got married, I watched endless chick flicks and dreamed of happily ever after. No one told me about the hard moments when the laundry needs to be done, you both have the flu, and the dog just peed on the carpet. But that's reality. When it comes to our dreams, we do much the same thing. We have a grand vision in which we ride off into the sunset with the desire of our hearts, and then we're disappointed when just over the next ridge, there's road construction and smog.

Yes, God-sized dreams are beautiful.

Yes, they're worth pursuing.

But they're not all cotton candy and daisies.

There are some things I wish someone had told me about dreams before I got started. And so, my friend, I'm going to share them with you.

Disclaimer #1: You Will Never Feel Ready

We tend to think in terms of 100 percent in our culture. We like the idea that we can do enough planning and preparing to make whatever outcome we desire a sure thing. It feels less risky that way. The danger comes in that we can delay forever in the name of being "responsible." Sometimes this relates to our circumstances—we want the weather to change, the crisis to pass, the leader to get on board with our idea. Other times it's more about who we are—we need more education, more experience, a better spiritual life. We start those requirements with the biggest dream-killing four-letter word of all: "When . . ."

Here's a secret: most dreams don't die a crash-and-burn death. If you at least try, then you're likely to have some kind of success come out of what you do.

Most dreams just never get born.

One weekend my husband and I visited a local community farm for their first day of planting. The organizers handed out packets of seeds. I dropped the seeds into my enormous purse with good intentions of planting them as soon as I got home. We became busy with other things and the seeds went untouched.

Every few days I would think about the seeds and how I should plant them. Then days turned into months and the opportunity slipped by without me even noticing.

Our dreams can be like those seeds. We carry them around with us and tell ourselves that we're going to plant them. Then life gets busy, distractions come, and we keep putting off what we know God has called us to do.

Yes, there are times for waiting and proactively seeking God's voice. But when we already know what he's asked us to do, it's time to plant. "Sow your seed in the morning, and at evening let your hands not be idle, for you do not know which will succeed, whether this or that, or whether both will do equally well" (Eccles. 11:6).

Don't wait until the time feels right. Don't wait until you feel ready. *You will wait forever.*

You don't have to be ready. Conditions don't have to be perfect. Because it's not about you. It's about God fulfilling his purposes through you, and he has always been able to make that happen in spite of our humanity and the fallen world around us.

If David had waited to feel ready, he would never have fought Goliath as a shepherd boy with a sling.

If Moses had waited to feel ready, he would never have led an entire nation to the Promised Land.

If Esther had waited to feel ready, her people would have perished at the hands of a wicked man.

When we don't feel ready, God has the opportunity to get the most glory.

Now, I'm not talking about being reckless and irresponsible. This is not an excuse not to pray or plan like we talked about in the chapter before this one. You need to put in the work and spend time listening to God's voice. But at some point it's the moment to act. We are to make our plans and step out in faith. Even if we

I look at the days ahead and wonder what they hold.

Don't we all?

And then these words:

"Go in the strength you have. . . . Am I not sending you?" (Judg. 6:14)

We don't have to . . .

wait to overcome our weaknesses,

complete the ten-point improvement plan,

figure everything out.

The strength we already have is all the strength we need.

Because we have a limitless God within us who loves us.

As is.

And he promises to stick by us.

All the way.

don't fully go the right direction, God can redirect us to end up where he wants us to go.

You don't have to be ready for anything.

You only have to be ready for the next step God has for you to take.

And you are.

Disclaimer #2: You Will Not Like Your Dream Sometimes

Like that day my husband discovered me curled up on the couch bemoaning my dream, there will be times when you feel like you'd rather be doing anything *but* your dream. When this starts happening to me, I have fantasies about running off to New Zealand to become a Starbucks barista. I can barely make a cup of black coffee, much less a triple-shot grande no-whip mocha, but when I get tired of my dream I become a bit delusional.

Now, feeling like this doesn't mean you don't love your dream. It doesn't mean that it isn't what God called you to do after all. It doesn't mean you messed up or heard wrong or any of the things the enemy would like you to believe.

It's just part of living out a dream in a fallen world.

You see, we're made for two places: Eden and heaven. I'm not sure where you are at this moment, but I can guarantee it's not either of those. While we don't get to live in those places right now, we still have the ability to capture a bit of both in our imaginations. Eden reminds us of *who we're created to be* and heaven reminds us of *where we're called to go*. God said he has "set eternity in the human heart" (Eccles. 3:11), and I think our ability to dream is a reflection of that truth. We can create visions far beyond what's possible in this world. Their beauty pulls us forward, excites us, causes us to press in deeper to Jesus. Believing that there is something more keeps us going when life can be hard.

This near-perfect dream is always the best place to start because it pulls us the farthest and the highest. Yet when we turn that dream into a set of expectations that everything *must* be that way right here, right now, then we're headed for disillusionment.

The most important part of the desires of your heart will come into being. The essential aspects of your God-sized dreams will happen. But they will not look like that picture-perfect vision that you started with in the first place.

I go to a lot of baby showers. Cute little presents like bibs and pacifiers get passed around. Even diapers are built into fake cakes and declared "Adorable!" A few months after the baby comes, the diapers are anything but adorable and that mama is wiping spit-up off that sweet little bib for the tenth time. Imagine if you said, "Well, you look pretty tired and like you're not exactly enjoying this at the moment. That baby must have been a bad idea." She'd promptly kick you out the door and tell you her baby is the cutest thing in the universe, thank you very much.

Yet we don't often extend the same kind of grace when it comes to our dreams. We start out at the "baby shower" stage when it seems everything is going to be perfect. Then we hit the sleepless nights and changing diapers phase and call it quits because surely if this was our dream, it wouldn't be so hard and we'd love every minute.

If you don't love *any* minute of your dream, then that's a concern. But having days when you don't like that dream all that much and you'd like to trade it in for a convertible and a beach house is totally normal.

There's nothing wrong with you.

There's nothing wrong with your dream.

There's just a whole lot wrong with this fallen world. And for now, that's where we get to live out our dreams.

When you have those moments, just remember they will pass. You will get through this time. There will be better, brighter days ahead.

Sometimes we do drift away from our dream in a way that wears us out on a long-term basis. For example, a woman has a great job as a music teacher. She loves the kids and the creativity. She does so well at it that she's offered a promotion to head up a new initiative in the district that will take the music programs in the schools to a new level. She jumps at the opportunity, and six months later she finds herself dreading going to work each day. What happened? No kids and no creativity. This new job seemed to be her dream, but it wasn't. Beware of parallel or imitation dreams. Know the core characteristics of your dream and stay as close to them as possible—even if moving away from them seems enticing because of other benefits.

If you've gotten away from what you're truly called to do, then realign and get back to where you started. This is more than an occasional bad day, frustration, or needing to push through a hard time. And if that's the case, then it's time for some adjusting.

You won't always like your dream. But you will always love it. Somewhere deep inside you, there will still be that whisper that says, "Even if you're tired, even if this doesn't seem worth it, even if you feel like you're crazy, *this* is what you've got to keep doing somehow."

The good news? Just like in a good marriage, wait a bit and the spark will come back. You'll open your eyes one morning and all of those old feelings will be there again. And you'll be so glad you stayed.

Disclaimer #3: You Will Sometimes Feel Alone

She confesses over the phone, "I spent time with some women in my neighborhood last night. They all talked about normal things—the weather, kids, which restaurants were good. Then they asked about my dream, so I took a deep breath and told them my latest idea. It got so quiet you could hear the crickets. Then someone said, 'That sounds exciting!' and changed the subject."

When we're captivated by a calling, it takes over our lives. We eat, sleep, and breathe it. Our passion and energy for it are endless. We're enthralled by every new detail, every little development. It becomes part of who we are. Then if other people don't respond in the way we'd like to what's on our hearts, it can feel as if we're being personally rejected.

But no one will ever love your dream the way you do.

We talked about this a bit in the last chapter, but it's important enough to touch on again. This dream is *your* baby. No one else cares what color its poo was that morning or how many ounces it had at every one of the last ten feedings. Yes, they want to hear some of the stories and hold it occasionally. They want to see the birthday party snapshots and congratulate you when it goes off to college. But you are the one raising this dream.

Don't take it personally when other people aren't as interested or supportive as you'd like for them to be. They love you. They want to be there for you. They most likely have good intentions.

A dream only lives in one heart. "Each heart knows its own bitterness, and no one else can share its joy" (Prov. 14:10). Other people literally can't feel what you do, experience it the way you can, see the vision the way you do.

Because they love you, they will try. Some will try very hard. But at the end of the day, it's unrealistic to expect them to be as excited as you are about this dream.

Sometimes you may even have outright opposition. You might have a "Pharaoh" in your life who refuses to let the dream happen, like Moses did.

But usually that's not what discourages us the most. The moments that can threaten to derail us from our dream completely are usually when we feel simply and quietly alone.

Elijah had a moment like that after a major showdown with the prophets of Baal in the Old Testament (see 1 Kings 18–19). God shows up in a serious way and then Elijah hightails it to the desert, tells God he's done, and declares, "I'm the only one . . ." (see 19:10). While we may vary in the ways we finish that sentence, those four words are a sure sign for all of us that our hearts need some TLC. God tells Elijah that's he's far from the only one, and the same is true for us too. But in those moments, the isolation can feel very real.

You are not alone. I am not alone. We are not alone.

But we will all have moments when it feels that way. That doesn't mean there's anything wrong with you. God didn't rebuke Elijah—he fed him and let him rest. Sometimes feeling alone means we're exhausted and we need to take time to care for ourselves.

Sometimes feeling alone means we're the person God has chosen to carry this out. While we're called to be in connection with others, there are lots of examples of when God gave an individual a particular assignment only he or she could complete. When that happens, we feel weird because we end up doing something like building an ark in the front yard.

One of the most important tests of your dream is your ability to push through those times when you feel alone or strange and finish what God has called you to do anyway.

God doesn't think like we do, and if you're following his plans, there will be times when it seems you are completely out of step with everyone else. Good for you. Just keep going.

We as dreamers can sometimes add to this by not sharing the dream fully or effectively with others in our lives. We spend a lot of time in our own minds wondering about what to do next and how that will work out and picturing the future. We come back from those journeys assuming everyone else in our lives has been on that path too. But they haven't. It's up to us to hone our skill of sharing our dreams with those who are closest to us. If we don't share the vision, they can't join us as we move forward. Yes, there are inherently times when we'll feel alone no matter what, but we can lessen those by intentionally making others part of our dream too.

Sometimes we feel alone not because we need to be with others but because God wants to be with us. Our lives are busy—especially when we're pursuing a dream—and God may want to pull us aside for a bit. We've been going one hundred miles an hour on a racetrack surrounded by other cars, and all of a sudden we find ourselves parked in a quiet corner. That doesn't mean we've messed up. Instead it's often God's way of saying, "I've got something important to tell you" or "I need to prepare you for the next part of the race."

God is always with us, so that means even when it feels like it, we're never really alone. Sometimes the feeling that we are alone is actually an invitation to stop and recognize his presence with us.

You will feel alone at times. But you don't have to be lonely.

You're surrounded by love more than you can see, more than you'll ever fully know.

(A little note from me: I've started doing e-coaching to help God-sized dreamers feel less alone. You can find out more at www.holleygerth.com.)

Disclaimer #4: Success Will Look Different Than You Think

When we start down the path of our dream, we have an idea of what the "gold medal" we'll receive when we cross the finish line will look like. Maybe we want to write a *New York Times* bestselling book. Maybe we want to have a thousand people attend our event. Maybe we just want to get our kids off to college without any of them going to jail.

We want to know that we did it right.

And for that to happen, we need to have some concrete, clear goals in mind.

But God, in his mysterious ways, hardly ever lets us have that kind of goal. He moves the finish line just before we think we're going to cross it. He changes up the course. He announces that we're doing a triathlon and not just a footrace.

He's not doing that to trick us, discourage us, or make us want to throw our hands in the air and quit. He's doing that so we remember that success is not about results. It's about a relationship. God is not all that interested in your getting things done. If he made the world in seven days, there's nothing he can't check off his to-do list without your help. What he wants on this journey to your dream is intimacy with you.

Success is simply this: obedience.

It's the moments when we forget this that we panic. That's when the parade of "have to's" start marching through our minds. I *have to* get this promotion or I'll be a failure. I *have to* make this company a success or I'll let everyone down. I *have to* reach that family goal or I'll look foolish.

With God, there aren't "have to's" involved. He gave us free will. With him, all of the steps of our dreams are "get to's." I *get to* take this promotion so I can make a bigger difference. I *get to* make this company a success so I'll have more resources to share with those in need. I *get to* reach this goal so I can glorify God.

Saying yes to God at every step is the only true success when it comes to your dream.

I've had a few moments when a really big dream of mine has come true. I feel joy, yes, and yet there's always this little whisper of *"Is this it?"* nagging in the back of my heart. That little whisper used to drive me crazy, but I've learned to recognize it as an important reminder that no, this isn't it. That success you're picturing in your mind might be wonderful, but it will not fulfill you. Only God can do so. And if you decide that the world's definition of success is the only one that you'll pursue, then you will fail even if you attain it because you will miss what matters most.

What fulfills us isn't the gold medal. It's the Maker of the universe.

There's a huge difference between setting goals and creating idols. Serve the One who loves you with excellence. But don't use him to serve your personal agenda. God is not a means to an end. He is the end.

He *is* the success you seek.

He is better than a *New York Times* bestselling book.

He is richer than millions in the bank.

He is the "more" that your heart is looking for in everything you pursue.

He promises, "You will seek me and find me when you seek me with all your heart" (Jer. 29:13). You're not called to pursue goals. You're called to pursue a Person. That's what dreams are really all about—going with God.

When you suddenly find more of him, then you know you've succeeded.

You might be spooning baby food into a little mouth and realize that the dream you prayed for is sitting in a high chair right in front of you.

You might get an email late at night saying, "I never told you that what you did made a difference to me, but . . ."

You might push through that last obstacle in a project to find you've finally broken new ground and now what matters most can grow.

Then all at once you feel his presence with you, a whisper inside your heart that seems to say, "Yes, you are a good and faithful servant." It's an echo and a preview of what we all hope to hear one day when we cross the only true finish line into heaven.

There's something more than a gold medal waiting for us. It's a crown we'll get to lay at the feet of the One who walked with us all the way.

If you don't achieve "success" in the way you imagined, don't despair. Most likely that was never God's goal for you. Whatever he has called you to do, he promises to complete through you. *If you are obedient, then you are successful regardless of the results.*

The most important "done" in your life is not the one you write next to your biggest goal. It's the one that will be spoken over you when you hear "well done" from the Lover of your soul.

Disclaimer #5: One Day This Dream Will Be Your New Normal

Stop and look around you for a moment. Wherever you are, there's probably a piece of a God-sized dream. It could be that the man sitting on your couch is the husband you asked God for years ago. The chaos in the other room could be the voices of the children you didn't know if you'd ever have. You could be on a flight for a job you asked God to give you. You might be at a church that you spent a long time looking for before settling in to one that felt like home.

When we're pursuing a dream, it feels all-consuming. It seems like this will be *the dream* forever. It's hard to even imagine having what our hearts long for, much less feeling like it's normal for it to be in our lives. Yet most of us are living right in the middle of many of our God-sized dreams from yesterday.

Our culture is big into finding *the* one or *the* calling or *the* dream. But it doesn't seem to work that way as much in the kingdom of God. Our lives with him are a journey, and he's always calling us forward to the next thing. "They go from strength to strength, till each appears before God in Zion" (Ps. 84:7). You will most likely go from dream to dream during your lifetime.

Yes, some dreams will be more meaningful than others. Some will consume years or even decades of your life. But believing that there's just one dream out there for you puts way too much pressure on it. The God-sized dream in your heart right now isn't *the only thing* God has for you—it's simply *the next thing*. He may bring it into being, and you'll get to set your feet firmly on that piece of Promised Land for a season. Or he might redirect you to something new, and you'll find that original dream isn't what he had in mind after all.

If you do make it to your God-sized dream, at first it all feels shiny and new. Every moment is a wonder. Every new opportunity is miraculous. Yet over time it simply becomes normal. Just like when we fall in love, our bodies can't sustain all the adrenaline and other chemicals that get our hearts pumping when we're in pursuit of a dream.

If you're in the phase of the dream when it's exciting and every day is filled with glory, then take time to savor and enjoy it. What many of us don't realize is that one of the best parts of the dream is the journey to it. Sometimes what happens along the way even turns out to be more meaningful and fulfilling than the end result we had in mind because of who we become and what we experience along the way. Savor those moments. Appreciate them. Don't let them be a blur as you zip past to what you think will truly make you happy.

Maybe you've actually achieved your dream and you're wondering why it isn't as exciting as it has been in the past. If so, just know that all dreams become our new normal after we've lived with them for a while. In this scenario, the key is to remember to stay grateful and to continue asking God what else he may have for us. We don't want to become too complacent or comfortable, and yet expecting the dream to always feel new isn't realistic.

You will continue to grow as a person throughout your lifetime, and that means your dreams will grow along with you. What challenged you yesterday may become easy at some point. What you thought you really wanted may turn out to be a stop along the road to somewhere else. The dream you thought would always be your passion may give way to another deeper call that surprises you when it appears.

You don't have to find or achieve "the one" when it comes to God-sized dreams. Expecting that to happen can keep you in a holding pattern forever. Just see each new dream as another step on the journey, another piece of the Promised Land God is calling you to possess. He may have you stay there for a while or move you on more quickly than you imagined. Like we talked about before, the "more" you are looking for isn't the dream itself. It's the Dream Giver.

Each new dream he places in your heart and has you pursue is an opportunity to know him in a different way. Maybe one dream reveals his faithfulness. Another shows you his strength. Then the next one helps you discover his infinite tenderness.

Dreams also show you more of who you are too. As you pursue different ones, you stretch, grow, and become even more of who you've always been created to be. Dreams are a sign that you're gloriously, beautifully awake to life. Stay that way even when your dream becomes your "new normal."

Remember how you pursued that dream.

Remember how you longed for it.

Remember that today you are living in the answered prayers and realized hopes of yesterday.

Conclusion

Dreams are unpredictable. We don't know where they'll take us, what will happen along the way, or where we'll wind up in the end. But in all of that uncertainty, there's One who is the same "yesterday and today and forever" (Heb. 13:8). He's the same One who said, "I am doing a new thing" (Isa. 43:19). What God does in your life will always be changing, always surprising. Who he is will always remain the same.

That's what gives us the courage to dream.

The disclaimers are never too much for the One who has claimed you as his own and called you on this adventure with him.

He's even better than happily ever after.

Go Deeper Guide

(Download a printable version with lines for writing at www.holley gerth.com on the "Books & More" page.)

1. What "seeds" of dreams are you carrying around in your pocket? Remember, this may not be the season for them, but at least you know they're there and can be planted in God's perfect timing.
2. Describe a time in your life when you realized a blessing in your life wasn't "perfect" after all (getting married, having a baby, starting a new job). How did you find the joy in it again?
3. Who in your life shares your God-sized dreams? If there's not anyone right now, who would you like it to be (a good friend, business partner, romantic relationship, etc.)? Begin praying for God to bring the people you need for this dream into your life.
4. What's your definition of success?
5. "They go from strength to strength, till each appears before God in Zion" (Ps. 84:7). What's "normal" in your life now that was once a God-sized dream (e.g., getting married, having children, pursuing a creative passion)?
6. Which "Disclaimer" in this chapter spoke to your heart most? What will you remember from it?
7. Are you discouraged about your dream? If so, write that down here. What's the truth you need to hear from God instead?

Dream It. Do It.

Make a list of the "God-sized dreams come true" in your life. They can be small or big. When has God answered your prayers? What blessings do you see around you that simply seem "normal" now? When we're pursuing a dream, we can lose sight of how many have already come true for us. Remembering can bring joy and encourage our hearts when we need it most.

7

When Your **God-Sized Dreams** Go Wrong

The first drip slips from the sky as thunder claps its hands above us.

We're in a park trying to shoot a video for my next book.

Hours of preparation have gone into this time.

Schedules have been rearranged. Props have been purchased.

Most of all, a vision has clearly been cast. We knew exactly how this was going to work out. We'd seen it in our minds a thousand times—now all that remained was bringing everything into reality.

Or so we thought.

That first drop is followed by another. Then another. Before we even fully realize what's happening, the sky cracks open and pours buckets on us. The water is like an invisible hand, covering everything, overflowing our paint cans, drenching a canvas where we'd been carefully creating.

We dash to our car, grabbing whatever we can to carry with us.

I pull the door tight behind me. *This is not the way I thought it would be,* I whisper to myself.

We take a break until the rain stops and come back to begin filming again. Work is redone. The vision resumes. And then just as it seems we're back on track, once more the sky has other ideas.

Colors run like a rainbow river onto the sidewalk. We take cover under a giant tarp, but as the storm rages on, it becomes clear we're done for the day.

Another dash to cars. Another reckless gathering of whatever we can salvage. My umbrella is small, and in the end I drop it.

I stand in the rain, soaking wet in a red dress, and I lift my hands to the sky. The only words that come to my mind are the last ones I expected.

This is the most fun I've had in a really long time.

Letting Go of Control

God-sized dreams can take over our worlds. That's true even when it's a relatively small dream, like that video. What starts out as a creative adventure full of freedom can quickly narrow down to worry about details, intricate plans, and what we think we must control.

Let me lean in and whisper a secret to you, my friend: *God-sized dreams are not controllable.* To believe any different is to tell yourself that a bucking bronco in the rodeo ring is no different than a sweet pony at the petting zoo.

The reason we can't tame our dreams is because the One who gives them to us is wild. We want God to be more predictable—especially when we're doing what we think he wants. That film was covered in prayers that it would all be "for God's glory and the good of his daughters." And yet it rained. Not just rain—*it poured.*

Why? Heaven only knows. I mean that literally. I have no idea why on a day when we worked so hard, prepared so much, and planned every detail, God saw fit to let all of it turn into puddles on the sidewalk.

If you dare to follow a God-sized dream, dare to try for anything more than ordinary in your life, dare to take a leap outside your comfort zone, then I can guarantee at some point the same will happen to you.

Because we don't have control.

Oh, we tell ourselves we do. Or if we don't dare say it out loud, then at least we live it. We do our best to construct a reality in which we know what happens next in the story. Sure, many times we should do so. It's part of practicing wisdom and stewardship.

But that is not the same as getting to write the story. We get to say yes to what the Author asks of us, yet inevitably we turn the page and what comes next is not what we had in mind at all.

When that happens, our minds quickly search for an explanation or someone to blame. That someone is often ourselves. We question, "What did I do wrong?" This seems to be especially true for visionaries because we can so clearly see what we think should be. When reality and our ideals collide, it always seems like our fault, that we fell short in some way. My friend, let me cup your brave, beautiful face in my hands and tell you that often that isn't so at all. It's simply because you're on a journey not with a tame lion, not with a mild-mannered author but with the One who flung stars into space, who spoke and there was light, who is weaving history together in a way we will never understand this side of heaven.

Let him have control.

Because here's the thing: *whoever is really in control is responsible for the results.* And as much as we may stamp our feet in the rain and whine about things not going the way we want, having the weight of what ultimately happens on our shoulders would be infinitely harder.

Our part is not control. It's not results. It's obedience. It's intimacy with the One who asks us to trust him even when nothing makes sense.

We all come to a place when we're standing in the rain watching everything we hoped for wash away. What do we do then? Do we raise our fists at the heavens? Or do we take off our shoes and dance in the puddles because we are standing on holy ground?

It's the choice we all must make. And the choice that ultimately makes us.

Trying Again

So what do you do if your God-sized dream gets derailed? Actually, I should reword that question: What do you do *when* your God-sized dream gets derailed? Because it will. Several times.

An old saying slips into my mind, and somehow it seems wiser as the years go by: if at first you don't succeed, try, try again.

There's nothing romantic about the notion of "trying again." We love the stories of heroes who scale Mount Everest on the first shot, who win the gold medal their first time at the Olympics. Yet even in those grandiose stories, there are thousands of "try agains" behind the scenes.

What I want to have an honest talk about here is the shame we feel in needing to "try again"—especially as Christians.

We place high expectations on ourselves. We feel "called" to do something and therefore certain that all will unfold just the way we imagine. And if it's not right, then we must be to blame.

Oh, that is a heavy load to carry, my friends. One that can weigh us down until we stop in the middle of the road to the Promised Land and say, "I can't do this anymore."

In every other area of our lives, it seems we're able to receive grace, to find freedom, to accept that the work God is doing in us won't be complete until heaven.

But our dreams? We'd better get it right the first time or we're disqualified.

Not so, my friend. The same "try again" grace that lets you get up and restore that relationship, renew that commitment, reach out once more for God's love is the grace that will be with you every step of this journey too.

It seems the enemy tries to keep us away from God-sized dreams in two ways. First, through so much fear that we never even start. But also by telling ourselves that unless we do it perfectly and everything unfolds according to plan, then this must not be God's will and we should just give up.

That's not true.

When we look through Scripture, the paths to dreams being fulfilled are full of zigzags and "try agains" along the way. David was anointed by the prophet Samuel and told he would one day be king. Yet the years that followed were filled with the current king, Saul, chasing him through the wilderness and attempting to take his life. Talk about a detour! Joseph got sold by his brothers and unjustly thrown into jail before becoming second to Pharaoh.

It's all about being faithful where we are and refusing to quit until we see the vision God has placed in our hearts become a reality.

The video that got ruined by the rain? Even as I write this we're trading emails about another shoot on another day. Try again. Will it work this time? I don't know.

What I do know is that there are two kinds of pain in this life: risk and regret. I'd rather live with the first than the second.

The path to your God-sized dream that you had in mind may not be turning out the way you want. You may wonder why God even chose you to walk it. You may feel like someone else should be in your shoes.

Listen closely: If you have heard the call, then you must go. God will make sure you get to where he wants you in the end.

Try, try again.

Changing Your Perspective

Sometimes the storm that comes into our lives isn't a passing summer shower that happens to put a dent in our plans for the day. Sometimes the red that flashes on the radar of our dreams is more like a hurricane, and we're left standing with shattered hopes by the time it passes.

In my first devotional book, *Rain on Me,* I shared about the storms in our lives. Those words came out of the personal storm my husband and I have faced for years—infertility. As I write, that rain has not relented even though it's been almost seven years.

But who I have become and how I respond to that rain is totally different than when our journey began.

We don't have a choice about the rain that comes into the pathway of our dreams, but we can choose what we do with it—*and what we let it do to us.*

When my Nana was twenty-nine years old, she contracted polio. She was barely clinging to life and told she would likely never walk again, and the outlook for her dreams seemed grim. A pastor came to visit her and said these simple words: "Frances, this can make you bitter or better." Years later she'd say with a smile on her face, "I chose better."

Perhaps you're just starting out in your dream and the thought of something going wrong isn't even on the horizon. I'd still challenge you: *decide now*. Decide now that no matter what happens you won't let bitterness in. Decide now that you will guard your heart. Decide now that your response to the rain will be to see that every drop can lead to growth.

Maybe the hard time has already come and you're wondering what to do now. *Press on*, my friend. You are going to make it. What seems like your greatest defeat may turn out to be your most shining victory when you look at it in the rearview mirror.

The day before the infamous downpour on our filming, a friend of mine and I met for coffee. We talked about some upcoming God-sized dreams and the fears that seemed to knock at the door of my heart each day about how it might all turn out.

"What's the worst-case scenario?" she asked.

I looked at her in shock and then slowly began to spill out all I'd been afraid to even think, much less say out loud. In the light, those monsters in the closet didn't seem so scary after all.

Then the next day at the filming, I found myself face-to-face with a real, live worst-case scenario. And it turned out to be just what I needed.

When we finally pulled away, soaking wet, I noticed four little girls laughing and jumping at the edge of the sidewalk, soggy pigtails flying through the air, broad smiles across their faces. I remembered doing the same earlier in life. Rain wasn't a nuisance but instead an opportunity on hot summer days.

I wondered when I stopped feeling that way, how I decided to start fighting the rain instead of realizing that it led to every flower I saw blooming around me.

The girls squealed with unexpected joy.

"It really is a matter of perspective," I whispered.

Guarding Your Heart

As the rain began to slip from the sky that day, we quickly decided what had to be protected and what could be left in the elements. Cameras, phones, and valuable papers quickly found refuge under a table or tucked into a car before anything else. Other items soaked in the torrent until we came back for them later.

When it seems our God-sized dreams begin to go wrong, we have a similar decision to make. What will we let bear the brunt of it? What will we hide away? In the middle of it all is our hearts.

"Above all else, guard your heart" insists Proverbs 4:23. "Guarding" can bring visions of locked doors and high security safes. But shutting our hearts completely means ceasing to dream as well.

In the time those words were written, guarding was done not by technology or highly sophisticated locks but instead by literal guards. Those guards decided who got in and who stayed out. Guarding was not a one-time, passive process but a proactive one that required being highly alert, engaged, and intentional. It's the same for our hearts, especially when things on the road to our dreams get hard.

As dreamers, we have hearts that naturally tend to swing open. We let in ideas, people, and opportunities. Through all of those, we piece together the vision it seems God has for our lives. Especially when we're young, the guards of our heart may be more like a welcoming committee. Hopefully, over time we learn to use more wisdom and discernment. We begin to ask what really belongs in that sacred space within us and what should be left outside.

Then something happens and we tell the guards to shut the place down. No one gets in, nothing gets out. We've tried to dream and we've learned it's anything but safe. Yet there, alone, in the quiet of our hearts we find that rather than feeling protected we begin to despair. Where is the life and growth? What's new? Where are we headed?

Our dreams can't coexist with absolute security. We can't eliminate risk and still have our God-sized dreams come true. It just isn't possible. A dream coming to pass always requires a leap between what is now and what could be.

So, yes, guard your heart, but don't lock it away—no matter how much you've been hurt, no matter how much it feels like doing so will guarantee your safety.

Learn from your hurt, but don't make it a lock on the door of your life.

To help guard your heart when it comes to decisions about your dreams, ask yourself:

- Does this align with Scripture?
- What do the wise people in my life say about it?
- When I pray about this, what does it seem God is whispering to me?

When the rain comes, protect what's valuable. But don't hide it away so deeply that it never sees sunshine again.

Dreams need light to grow—so do you.

Remembering It's Never the End

For forty days, water floods the earth. Noah and his family float on an ark, wondering what will happen next in the earth's story. Finally, a rainbow appears—a visual promise that God will never again flood the world. Yes, it will rain. But never again will the water overcome.

I believe that promise applies to us too. Standing in the park, it seemed to us that the storm would never stop, that we'd never be dry again. But it eventually blew over, our clothes found their way to the dryer, and we went on with our day. Eventually, we'll go on with our dream of that video being completed too.

Perhaps our rainbow is found in these words: "He who began a good work in you will carry it on to completion until the day of Christ Jesus" (Phil. 1:6). This verse doesn't say *if, might, maybe,* or *hope so*—it says the good work *will* be completed. Perhaps not in the way we plan. Perhaps not in the time we plan. Perhaps not even until heaven. But those desires in your heart? The ones you know are from God? They will be fulfilled. He's not teasing you, toying with your heart, making you long for something he doesn't intend to provide.

You will not be flooded by disappointment to the point you can no longer keep your head above water. You will not be washed away without God realizing what's happening.

You will make it through the rain. Your dreams will dry off, the sun will come out again, and you'll carry on with what God has placed within your heart. It's still there. It's safe within you. You may be soaking wet, but if you look closely, you'll find the deepest, most sacred part of your dream is still dry.

That's because it's protected not by you but by the One who placed it there in the first place. The Dream Giver is also the Dream Keeper.

I'm sitting in the corner of a coffee shop. Across the room, a group of teen girls are huddled together with their mentor. I look at them, so many dreams and storms ahead for those pink T-shirts and bright eyes.

One says, "Even when we don't understand what God is doing, we can still trust his promises." She's holding an invisible umbrella in the shape of those words. One day when she needs it most, she'll reach for it. The rain will fall, the water will rise, and she will be okay. Maybe she'll even dare to embrace the rain.

Perhaps that's the heart of what dreaming really is—the receiving of what comes and making it part of something more than what we thought could be.

Today's showers into tomorrow's flowers.

The girls laugh low, and it sounds like spring thunder whispering through the skies about good things to come.

I turn my eyes upward, and I remember again how it feels to dance in the rain.

Go Deeper Guide

(Download a printable version with lines for writing at www.holley gerth.com on the "Books & More" page.)

1. Think of a time when you released control of a situation in your life to God. What happened? What's in your life now that you might need to give to him too?
2. When something doesn't work out the way you plan, do you tend to give up or try again? What encourages you to persevere?
3. How are you guarding your heart as you pursue your God-sized dreams?
4. Think of a decision you need to make in your life and put it through this set of questions as practice:
    - Does this align with Scripture?
    - What do the wise people in my life say about it?
    - When I pray about this, what does it seem God is whispering to me?
5. Are you facing discouragement or disappointment in your life right now? What does your heart need from God and those around you to move forward?
6. None of us are meant to go through life's storms alone. Who will walk through the rain with you? Who are you doing the same for too?
7. Write out a short commitment below to never, ever give up on what God calls you to do.

Dream It. Do It.

Rainy days will come on the way to your God-sized dreams. So start preparing now. Write a letter to yourself with encouragement about what's true. Then seal it up, tuck it away for a rainy day, and open it when you need to remember what God spoke to you before the storms came.

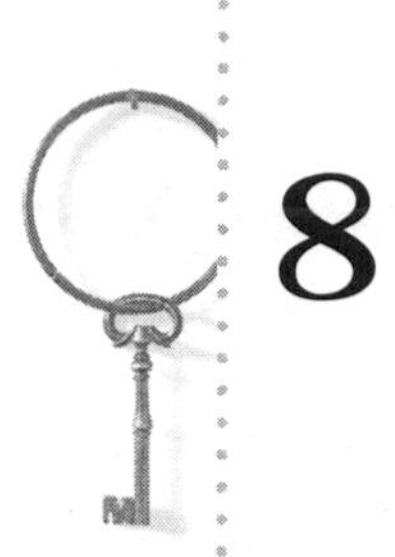

8

How to Stop Sabotaging Yourself

We've talked about how storms will come on the way to our God-sized dreams. But sometimes it's not life's weather that gets to us most—it's what we do to ourselves. God-sized dreams take a lot of energy, strength, and emotion. That means taking care of yourself as you pursue them is not self-indulgence or a luxury; it's a necessity. Believe me, I've learned that the hard way.

I remember a turning point years ago when tears slipped from my eyes. I was utterly exhausted. Working full-time, going to grad school, and keeping up with a heavy writing load had taken their toll on me. I felt as if I couldn't move forward one more step. *I know better,* I silently thought. *How did I get to this place?*

Even being trained as a counselor still wasn't enough to keep me from standing on the brink of burnout. Since that day several years ago, I've realized that most dreamers find themselves at this point at one time or another. *But you don't have to.* I made changes in my life that enabled me to pursue my God-sized dreams with joy, energy, and a full heart. So let's talk about the common mistakes and pitfalls that you can avoid as you're pursuing all God has for your life.

Remember You're Human

When we're caught up in a God-sized dream, we can forget that we all have limits. Our enthusiasm and passion can almost act as painkillers that dull us for a time to the emotional and physical toll our journey is taking on our minds, hearts, and bodies.

Yes, moving toward the "more" God has for you is an exhilarating process. But it also takes more energy and resources than any other season in our lives. My husband is an avid biker. One of the biggest thrills in his life is completing a challenging ride. Yet he knows that if he's unprepared for what's ahead, then his body won't be able to complete what his mind is determined to do. Bikers call this state "bonking." It's when your physical resources have been completely depleted, and even the most experienced and fit athlete can find himself or herself sitting bewildered on a curb with the finish line only a little bit farther down the road.

One of the most important lessons athletes in training learn is not just their strengths but also their limitations. When I first started joining my husband for bike rides, he repeated three words to me often: "Watch your pace." I had a tendency to start off at a high speed, fueled by the fun and exhilaration of the experience, but by the time I climbed the last hill, my mood was anything but enthusiastic. I realized I did much the same thing in other areas of my life. I would start a new dream, project, or strategy full of zeal only to find myself weak and weary before I reached my goal. I've learned the hard way that *everyone has limitations*. That's not a sign of weakness or failure but instead a reminder that we are gloriously and imperfectly human. While most of us roll our eyes and wish we could banish those limitations, they play an important role: to remind us that we're not God.

Actually, many of our limitations are intentionally placed there by him. He's the one who decided we'd all need an average of eight hours of sleep and frequent meals. When you look at humans as a species, it's clear we're not built simply for efficiency. We're not machines that can endlessly perform. We're not robots that are immune to the conditions around us. When God declared that what he made was good, it included the parts of your humanity that may sometimes frustrate you or slow you down.

Know your limitations. Embrace them. Then use them to get to your God-sized dreams. For example, when we work out with weights, there's a natural breakdown of our muscles—a limitation to what we can lift. But when those muscles are given rest after exercise, that tearing down is what enables new muscles to grow. If we take this into account and modify our behavior accordingly, that limitation ultimately leads us to greater strength. But if we ignore it, then we miss out on some gains our effort would otherwise bring.

You are not a superhero. You are not invincible. You are intentionally human. You don't have to be afraid that your limitations will keep God from accomplishing what he wants to do through you. Even Jesus grew tired, got thirsty and hungry, and had other human limitations. What does that tell us? *Being human is not a sin.*

God can and will accomplish all he wants to do in and through you. Your limitations won't prevent that—but pushing yourself to the point of burnout just might. Take care of yourself. Respect what you need. Accept being human.

You're loved just as you are by a limitless God who can more than make up for whatever you feel you lack. As Sara Frankl, an amazing woman who spent much of her life homebound and yet made a significant difference in this world, said, "There is such pressure to do everything to its limits, when all you need to do is do everything to YOUR limit . . . to the limit God gives inside of you."[8]

Take Care of Your Body

When we're on the journey to "more" in our lives, especially if it's a God-sized dream, the spiritual aspect of who we are can loom larger than anything else. But an important part of crossing the finish line well is purely physical. If you want a better, more fulfilled life and to achieve your dream, then you must take care of your body.

It's an odd thing about humans that we seem to consistently try to divide up parts of who we are. We think of our bodies as separate from what we consider to be the more meaningful parts of our existence. Yet throughout Scripture God consistently reflects the spiritual through the tangible. Jesus is described as "the Word made flesh" and this is just one example of how the physical is tied closely to God's heart for us.

Your physical condition matters when it comes to your God-sized dreams. Do you need to be an Olympic athlete? Nope. Not even close. But keeping up with the basics of eating fairly well and taking some time to move your body will do wonders as you pursue the path of all God has for you.

It's ironic that when we're in the midst of following a passion in our lives, we often grow tired, and the first things to go are usually what could actually make us feel better. Believe me, I know what it's like to skip out on exercise and choose the couch instead or reach for a candy bar rather than something healthier.

Only as I learned how those choices impact not just my waist size but more importantly my mental state did I start making small but consistent shifts in my behavior.

Our brains are fascinating. To me looking at how God has wired us is the equivalent of staring at the Grand Canyon. What he has created within us gives an astounding picture of his brilliance. It's important to know how he made us so that we don't unintentionally trip ourselves up in simple ways that can be avoided.

Like we talked about before, one area of our brains is in charge of emergencies. It takes over when we're in a fight-or-flight situation. God gave us this part of our minds so that when we need to act quickly and think later, we can effectively do so. In modern life we're not often chased by wild beasts, but everyday stresses have the same effect. We trigger this part of our brains and all we hear is "You must do something to feel better now!" So we reach for a doughnut, plop on the couch, or make another choice that later leaves us shaking our heads. As Laurel Mellin describes in *Wired for Joy*:

> Stress hormones affect your motivations, because you are in survival mode. Forget about compassion. Instead, you focus on surviving the moment, doing whatever it takes. In that stressed state, your thinking brain is not functioning well. It is not thinking magnificent thoughts and fueling you with passion to be your most altruistic self. Your emotions, thoughts, and behaviors are decidedly extreme, because even though you are not being chased by a hungry lion, your brain perceives that you are. Survival is the drive, and the chemical cascade is ensuring that you will do whatever you need to do to get what you want when you want it, without

> regard to how that affects others. That is the nature of the stress response.[9]

Stress is inherent in pursuing "more" in your life. It's part of God-sized dreams. When it's positive, stress serves as a motivator and pushes us toward growth (exercise is an example). But when we chronically live in stress, it saps us of our strength and we end up in survival mode.

Our brains have another area intended to help us rationally process life and our emotions. Most of the time, this is the part God intends to be in charge. But ensuring that happens means intentionally creating a healthy lifestyle. When we make poor food choices, ignore exercise, and don't get enough rest, then we flip ourselves into living out of a stress response. That makes it much harder to hear God's voice, love those around us, and effectively pursue the God-sized dreams in our hearts.

Again, this isn't about becoming an athlete. It's simply about removing unnecessary obstacles in our paths. Because they seem so ordinary and unglamorous, we can underestimate how much these little changes can impact us.

At a minimum:

1. *Commit to getting from seven to ten hours of sleep a night.* Don't buy into the myth that you don't have time to do what's needed—you always have time for God's will for you, and he created you to need that amount of sleep.
2. *Put a basic plan in place for healthy eating.* Keep it simple. I don't mean an extensive formula that includes fancy meals or extensive tracking. The easier you make it, the more likely you are to stick with it. For example, buy almonds instead of mini candy bars next time at the store. Keep healthy frozen dinners around for emergencies. Little changes can make a big difference.

3. *Get moving a few times a week.* Exercise is important for our physical well-being, but it's also a big part of what keeps us humming along mentally and emotionally as well. Research has shown that moderate exercise can be just as effective as an antidepressant because it releases natural feel-good chemicals in the brain. What exercise is the most fun for you? If possible, do that three times a week. One of my graduate school professors, Dr. Ryan Rana, liked to say that it's important to work as hard physically as we work mentally and emotionally or we get out of balance.

If you find yourself having a tough day, pause and ask, "What does my body need right now?" This may not seem like a spiritual question, but there are examples throughout Scripture like Elijah after the showdown with the prophets of Baal (he needed food and a nap; see 1 Kings 19:1–9), Jesus asleep on the boat with his disciples, and other times when what that individual needed most was something simple and tangible. Start there, because it will help you deal with whatever else may be happening.

Don't be surprised if you ask yourself that question and the answer that comes back is, "I need a triple-shot mocha with extra whipped cream." That's the part of your brain that's in charge of the stress response simply telling you what it thinks will make it all better *now*. Think of it like a toddler and kindly respond, "Thanks for that idea, but I think we'd better go with something different this time." Give yourself, and your brain, grace in those moments. Overall it serves you well—you just can't let it take charge in times of stress.

Think of your body as the vessel for the rest of you. Take care of yourself physically and respect your tangible needs. You're fearfully and wonderfully made, so learning to work with, rather than against, your body makes a big difference when it comes to your God-sized dreams.

Simplify Your Life

In *You're Already Amazing*, I talked about how we all have an emotional bank account. Much like our financial account, we make deposits and withdrawals. In that book, we discussed negative withdrawals and what to do about them. In our conversation now, we're still talking about withdrawals—but this time they're positive.

One of the reasons so many people burn out after being successful or achieving a dream is that they think because they love what they're doing and feel a great deal of passion that it's not going to take a toll on them. But any amount of energy and emotion given out is still expenditure, whether it's something that brings joy or sorrow.

I remember sitting in a class for my graduate degree in counseling and staring at a diagram about change in wonder. Although I don't recall all the details, it clearly showed how negative change (for example, losing a job) and positive change (for example, getting married) both cause stress. Timothy Ferris explains the difference:

> There are two separate types of stress. . . . Distress refers to harmful stimuli that make you weaker, less confident, and less able. Destructive criticism, abusive bosses, and smashing your face on a curb are examples of this. These are things we want to avoid. Eustress, on the other hand, is a word most of you have probably never heard. Eu-, a Greek prefix for "healthy," is used in the same sense in the word "euphoria." Role models who push us to exceed our limits, physical training that removes our spare tires, and risks that expand our sphere of comfortable action are all examples of eustress—stress that is healthful and the stimulus for growth.[10]

The goal isn't to avoid stress but instead to realize that both kinds cause withdrawals from our emotional and energy accounts.

What does this mean for your God-sized dream? You have made a decision to designate emotional and energy funds in a specific way. That naturally means that there is less to go around elsewhere. Just like most of us don't have unlimited bank accounts, our internal resources have limits as well (and as we talked about earlier, God created us this way).

Each time you spend a dollar on one thing, you are saying yes to that purchase and no to many other ways you could have used your money.

When you say yes to a God-sized dream, you are committing to a significant investment in your life. That means cutting back on extraneous emotional and energy expenses in other areas. Because many dreamers are big-picture idealists (which serves us well in many ways), we often underestimate the "cost" of what we're undertaking. Jesus put it this way: "Suppose one of you wants to build a tower. Won't you first sit down and estimate the cost to see if you have enough money to complete it? For if you lay the foundation and are not able to finish it, everyone who sees it will ridicule you, saying, 'This person began to build and wasn't able to finish'" (Luke 14:28–30).

These verses are talking about the cost of being a disciple. And, ultimately, that's what we're talking about too. This isn't just going after the "more" you want in your life—instead this is about saying yes to God and following him faithfully through God-sized dreams. There is always a cost.

Is it worth it? Oh yes.

But being able to finish well means, as Jesus says above, understanding the cost and planning for it ahead of time.

When I work with life coaching clients, I often give them the assignment to "say a hard no" during the week. In other words, to turn down something they feel pressured to do in order to pursue something more significant instead. It always makes them squirm a bit, but when they report back about what they chose to say "the hard no" to, there is always relief in their voice.

What is draining your time, emotions, or energy?

It can be as obvious as clutter in your house.

Or as complicated as a toxic relationship.

Whatever it is, now is the time to deal with it.

Make a list of everything that takes valuable resources that you will need for your God-sized dream. Everything. Put a minus sign (–) by anything that drains you and a plus sign (+) by anything that adds to your inner account by bringing you joy. Then look through the minuses and decide which things have to stay (for example, laundry) and which ones can be decreased, delegated, or eliminated all together (for example, the committee you signed up for that sucks the life out of you but you feel obligated to continue).

Look at the items that remain and begin to make plans for dealing with each one. For example, can someone help you with the laundry, or can you do it on one particular day? As you try to find solutions, you'll hear all kinds of nonsense in your mind: "You're selfish. Everyone else seems to handle this; why can't you?" Recognize those statements for what they are: lies that distract you from God's calling in your life.

You are giving God, those you love, and yourself a tremendous gift by simplifying your life so that you can focus on what matters most. It's actually the most unselfish thing you can do. Start by counting the cost, and you are much more likely to finish well.

Building Your Dream Team

From the very beginning, God made it clear that "it's not good for man to be alone" (or woman either) (see Gen. 2:18). Yet in our culture chasing a dream is often seen as a solitary pursuit. Let's put that myth to rest right now. No one achieves their God-sized dreams alone. Even Jesus had disciples, and he was perfect. We're not intended to carry out God's plans for our lives without the support and encouragement of others.

When it comes to God-sized dreams, it helps to fill several specific roles.

A Mentor

There's nothing new under the sun, and wherever you're going, someone else has already been there. Find someone who has pursued the dream that you have who can offer wisdom along the way. Or, if their journey isn't the same path as yours, at least look for someone who has experience doing what it takes to complete a dream well: taking risks, building relationships, persevering. Even if they're not in the same field as you are, those skills will transfer over to your situation too. Most importantly, a mentor is someone who follows hard after God with all of her heart and will remind you to do the same.

An Encourager

While a mentor is a few steps ahead of you, an encourager is someone who's right by your side. Your journeys are somewhat parallel, and she understands where you are now. You're facing the same kind of struggles, celebrating similar victories, and when one of you has a bad day, the other can be a source of strength. "Two are better than one, because they have a good return for their labor: If either of them falls down, one can help the other up. But pity anyone who falls and has no one to help them up" (Eccles. 4:9–10).

A "Younger" Woman

When Scripture encourages older women to train the younger, we tend to think of it in terms of age. But I think it's really more about the heart. When I use the term *younger*, I'm not referring to years but instead to where each woman is on her journey. She may just be starting out in her dream while you're midway through yours. Perhaps she wants to grow in an area where you have experience. Or her spiritual faith might be just taking root while yours has gone a little deeper. Who can benefit from where you are now?

A Cheering Section

In addition to the individuals above, thriving in your dream also comes from having a group of people you can turn to for encouragement, advice, or prayers. This can take time to build, but you can begin asking God, "Who is in my cheering section?"

As I tackled a challenge, my life coach, Denise Martin, admonished me to set up an "advisory board." These women serve as a team who can review ideas, confidentially pray, and speak the truth to me no matter how hard it may be for me to hear at times. I love that each one brings a different perspective, and their variety of strengths fills important gaps for me.

I communicate with my advisory board primarily through email. You can connect with yours online, over the phone, or face-to-face.

If you think, "I don't know who I would ask to be on my team," you're not alone. Most people don't have a group like this in their lives. And we all go through seasons and circumstances, such as a move, that impact our relationships at times. If you have even two people in your life you can confide in, including family members, that's more than most Americans, according to research.[11] Cultivating these kinds of relationships takes time and intention but is definitely worth the investment.

Who You DON'T Need

Each of the relationships above can help you as you pursue your dream. But before we wrap up this section, we need to talk about the kind of people you *don't* need in your life on this journey too. That may sound a bit harsh, but as we talked about before, the funds in your emotional and energy bank account need to be spent on your dream, and some people will drain away those resources without any real benefit to you or them.

Avoid negative people as much as possible. They will shoot holes in your dream, get you discouraged, and distract you with problems you can't fix. If you're around someone negative, intentionally resist the pull in that direction. Consistently go back to positive topics and tones in the conversation. You can't afford to spend your valuable emotion and energy, and even though they don't realize it, neither can they. You're doing those negative folks a favor by brightening their day a bit rather than joining the downward spiral.

Be ready for the doubters. Many people will tell you that your dream is silly or foolish or will never work. Take those statements as compliments and proof that you're disrupting the status quo—which is what every God-sized dream does. You don't want everyone to like your idea. If they do, it's not out of the box enough.

Change scares people, and the reaction they have is not about you but instead about their discomfort. Smile, nod, and move ahead.

Stand guard against bullies. One step past the doubters stand the bullies—those who intentionally oppose your dream. Again, if you've got bullies, it's a pretty good sign that you're doing something significant. Jesus definitely had his share. In *The Dream Giver*, Bruce Wilkinson says this about bullies:

> Some bullies you absolutely have to convince in order to move forward, especially if it's a boss or a key player in your Dream. . . . Some bullies simply need to know that you have heard them out. Some need to be affirmed for their viewpoint or role in your life. Some simply need to be avoided.[12]

In other words, expect bullies at some point and then strategically address them. It's not fun to engage with them, but ultimately they will help you build your perseverance.

Relationships are at the heart of who we are and all we do. While dreams can seem to be about tasks or achievements, ultimately they are always about people. That's because God is inherently relational. He *is* love, and whatever he calls us to do will be about love too.

Decide to Be on Your Side

What if our thoughts about ourselves were broadcast to the world? Are you getting chills down your spine just thinking about it? Me too! The reality is, most of us are much kinder to others than we are to ourselves. It's easy to offer grace to those who fail us, but when we don't meet our own expectations, we can be unmerciful. But in addition to the folks we talked about above, another essential member of your team is *you*.

A famous quote says, "We have seen the enemy and he is us." While we talked about bullies, it often turns out that we are our biggest opponent. Before we can move forward with all God has for our lives, we have to decide that we will be on our side.

The apostle Paul asks a rhetorical question, "If God is for us, who can be against us?" (Rom. 8:31). It seems the answer is intended to be "no one." Yet as I looked at those words one day, the realization flashed across my mind that there is someone who can be against me. It's *me*. I know that firsthand because I've struggled with being hard on myself throughout my life. I sometimes wonder if that's part of being a dreamer—because we can imagine everything as better (including ourselves), we become frustrated when the ideal isn't met.

So let's have a talk, you and I. It's time to stop coming against us and instead stand with God as we say, "I'm not perfect but I'm deeply loved, made in God's image, and I have everything I need to be all he's called me to be."

Occasionally a life coaching client will make a statement about herself that's so harsh it shocks me. I catch my breath and then quietly ask the question, "Would you say that to your dear friend?"

She quickly responds, "No, of course not."

I gently reply, "Then God doesn't want you to say it to yourself either." There's usually a moment of quiet as what this really means sinks into her heart.

When you wound yourself with your words, it's the same to God as if you were to doing it to someone else in your life. Jesus said to love our neighbors as ourselves. That means all of the "one another" statements in Scripture (i.e., be kind to one another, encourage one another) apply in our relationship with ourselves too.

We often fear that pride will creep in if we start treating ourselves with more kindness. But research has shown that those with a healthy self-relationship are more likely to be loving to others as well. Humility is strength under control. It's knowing who we are, being secure in that, and then choosing to serve.

You will face a lot of tough moments on the road to your God-sized dreams. Obstacles will appear, mistakes will be made, and sometimes you will be staring at the ceiling in the middle of the night and asking yourself, "Why in the world did I ever decide to do this?" It's at these moments when all of your encouragers are fast asleep that you need to be able to be on your own side and push through to what's next. More dreams die by self-inflicted wounds than any other kind.

God is for you . . . and it's time for you to be too.

Conclusion

There's only one way for the unique God-sized dream in your heart to come into being, and that's through you. God doesn't have a backup plan. You are here at this time, in this place for a purpose that only you can fulfill.

When we think of our dreams, it's easy to shift the focus outside of ourselves. We plan, strategize, and take steps forward. Yet what's most crucial to our dream is what's happening within. Taking care of yourself is not a luxury when you're pursuing a dream—it's a necessity. It's not selfish—it's the ultimate in self-discipline. You and everyone else in your life will benefit when you proactively address the areas of your life that have the potential to trip you up or slow you down.

You matter. You are wonderfully made. You are the vessel for a God-sized dream.

And that, my friend, is a beautiful thing.

Go Deeper Guide

(Download a printable version with lines for writing at www.holley gerth.com on the "Books & More" page.)

1. How is your pace of life right now? We all have one that's optimal. Does it feel like you're below it, above it, or just right? What changes might you need to make?
2. What are you doing to take care of your body (sleep, exercise, what you eat)? What's one small way you can do so even more? In other words, what does your body need right now?
3. If you haven't already, make a list of everything that takes valuable resources that you will need for your God-sized dream. Everything. Put a minus sign (–) by anything that drains you and a plus sign (+) by anything that adds to your inner account by bringing you joy. Then look through the minus column and decide which things have to stay (for example, laundry) and which ones can be decreased, delegated, or eliminated all together.
4. Who is on your dream team (mentor, encourager, younger woman, cheering section)? Note: if you don't have all of these people, it's okay. Most of us don't. Just begin praying for God to fill in the gaps.
5. What are you most critical of yourself about? What does God want to replace those words with instead?
6. In what other ways could you be sabotaging yourself? What changes can you make so that's no longer the case?
7. "If God is for us, who can be against us?" (Rom. 8:31). The answer to that question is intended to be "no one." Write a

short prayer to God expressing that you will side with him in being for yourself too.

Dream It. Do It.

Make plans to connect with someone on your dream team this week. Share an update about what's going on with your God-sized dream and let that person know how they can pray for you. Then ask how you can do the same for her too.

9

Why Your Dream Is Worth It

The sun had just begun to slip lower in the sky. I felt traces of sand between my toes as I stepped onto the narrow boardwalk that led to the beach. As I crested a dune, I took in a scene that caused tears to spring to my eyes. Standing on the beach in what felt like a glimpse of heaven were the writers of (in)courage, a website I co-founded. As I looked at them laughing and talking while they watched the sunset, all the hard moments of the last year flashed before me again. I caught the eye of co-founder Stephanie Bryant, and we smiled at each other, silently saying, "Yes, it's all been worth it."

As I reflected on that moment, I realized it was the closest I'd come to experiencing what it might be like to step into eternity and hear those words, "Well done, good and faithful servant." I knew all the struggles and battles of this life would fade away as I looked at the One I loved and whose joy I could now share forever.

God-sized dreams are always worth it for so many reasons—some that we experience in this life and others that wait for us in eternity.

Because God Doesn't Have a Plan B for You

If someone else has a dream similar to ours, we may think that there are other ways this dream can come into being. Surely someone else could take it on or do what you're called to do. But it's clear—there's just one irreplaceable you. God doesn't have a backup plan for your life. Either this dream happens through you or it doesn't happen at all. Yes, he can find another way to accomplish his purposes, but it won't be the same.

You are here at this time in history, with the strengths you have and the experiences you've gained, for a purpose. Every part of your life has been designed so that you can say a loud "Yes!" to God when he asks you to step out in faith with him.

As we talked about before, this isn't about the size of your dream. It may be as small as a mustard seed, but we know that in God's hands even just that much faith can move mountains. It's not what the world thinks, how much recognition we receive, or the amount of applause we hear that matters. More is not better in God's kingdom. Simply being obedient to whatever he asks matters most.

Because you are the only one who can fulfill this dream, there is no one better than you to do it. Resist the urge to compare, and instead embrace that this dream is between you and God. He doesn't want you to change who you are to be someone else. He simply wants you to become all he's created you to be and trust that means you will have everything you need to make this dream come true.

You've got something to give.

Something good and right and true.

Something fashioned in heaven and placed in your heart.

Something we need. And it's beautiful.

Maybe it's a smile.

A little kindness.

That dream you're ready to start living.

You matter.

Oh, how you do.

The God who flung stars into place, who holds the world in his hands, who makes all things possible lives in you.

And this week will be better because of what you two do together.

Watch out, world—
here comes you . . .

We need you, just you, to be who you are. We don't get a second chance at what you have to offer. We never have another opportunity to receive what you have to give.

You are one-of-a-kind wonderful. You are chosen by God for a particular purpose, and he promises to see it through to completion if you'll only say yes to what he's whispering to your heart—and your heart alone.

Because You Will Never Feel Closer to God Than When You're Pursuing a Dream

God-sized dreams are invitations for you to get on board with him and go to places your heart has never imagined. And there's only one way to get there—by being right by his side. The moments in my life when I've sensed God's presence most have always been when I'm taking a step of faith with him. That's true in Scripture all the way back to the Israelites' journey to the Promised Land. God's presence was with them, and their number one job was simply to follow wherever he led.

In our culture, we value learning and thinking quite a bit. We can find ourselves in the middle of a Christian life that's all about knowing. Yet somewhere within us there remains a longing to be *doing* with God. We're created not just for belief but also for action. When you put into practice what God has been whispering to your heart, it's the difference between talking about ice cream and sticking your spoon into the most delicious hot fudge sundae ever imaginable. There's simply no substitute for experience.

If your spiritual journey has been feeling a bit dull, then a deep dive into an adventure with Jesus might be just what you need. Don't wait until you feel like you know everything. You're going with the One who knows it all. He will fill you in as you go, through his Holy Spirit.

When James said, "Come near to God and he will come near to you" (4:8), he offered a powerful invitation. The more we pursue God, the more he chases us right back. We're made to share a life with him that's full of intimacy, excitement, and passion.

You are in a relationship with the God who spoke the world into being, who hung the stars in place, who created that dream in your heart. You may have many opportunities in your lifetime, but none is better than this—to let God take you by the hand and lead you into all he has for you.

In the classic story *Chariots of Fire*, Olympic runner Eric Liddell is planning to go to China as a missionary. But he first competes in the Olympics. When his sister questions this decision, he replies that yes, he will be a missionary, but that God also made him fast and he feels God's pleasure when he runs.

Find the moments when you feel God's pleasure, when you sense him right next to you urging you on, when your dream and your relationship with him intertwine in a flow that feels like what you've been made for all along. Then live in those moments as much as possible.

Because Dreams Make You Come Alive

We all know what it's like to simply go through the motions. We get up, move through our day, and drift off to sleep wondering if there's more to life. And no matter how much we try to silence it, something within us says, "Don't be satisfied with this." We brush it off and tell ourselves we need to be content. But the longing remains.

Then one day we find the courage to say yes to the whisper within us and what we're being asked to do. We take the first step of faith and find that rather than falling, we suddenly feel like we're flying. Parts of who we are that have been dormant, perhaps for years, spring to life again. We discover we can do more than we thought we could in ways we might not even have imagined.

Rather than an obligation, life begins to feel like an adventure. We wake up in the morning and want to know what God is going to do in and through us today. We drift off to sleep dreaming about what comes next. Even in the hard moments, there's still the exhilarating feeling that we are fully engaged in the world around us and we are right where we are supposed to be.

There's a myth in Christian culture today that says the Promised Land is only heaven. When I look through those chapters in Scripture, I just don't see that being true. Yes, the ultimate Promised Land is ours when we step from this life to the next, but I believe God has so much for us right here and now too.

We are made for a purpose, and until we are intentionally pursuing it, we feel half alive. We are dreamers waiting for someone to wake us up so the real adventure can begin.

If you feel numb, depressed, or even just flat-out bored, I don't believe that's God's plan for you. Yes, we all have seasons when we go through grief or experience difficulties. But if we live year after year in a state of just surviving, God has more for us. He didn't put you on this earth just so you could hold on by your fingernails until you get to heaven. He loves you and wants you to thrive. As one of my favorite verses says, "The LORD be exalted, who delights in the well-being of his servant" (Ps. 35:27).

But we have to agree with God that not only is this possible but it's actually what he wants for us. The Israelites wandered in the desert for forty years because they refused to believe God really could give them more. They looked at the Promised Land, saw the abundance, and said that they were better off playing it safe.

Don't settle. Don't give in to fear. Don't stand on the edge of all God has for you and be sent back to the desert.

You're allowed to be happy.

You're allowed to be blessed.

You're allowed to live a full life.

Even more than allowed—this is what God ultimately wants for you. If you believe anything else, then you have been sold a lie. Now let me be clear: all of the above doesn't come through doing whatever we want. That's not the way it works. But obedience is supposed to lead to joy. Even Jesus endured the cross "for the joy set before him" (Heb. 12:2). Don't let the idea that suffering is part of the Christian life trick you into believing that it's the entirety of what God has for you. It's not even the majority. It's only a gateway that he will use to bring you into deeper joy in the end.

And just surviving is certainly not God's plan for your life either. He didn't put you on the earth to be mediocre. He didn't form you with his hands, dream you up in his heart, and place you in this world for a purpose just for you to go through life being "fine."

Oh no, my friends. God has more for you—so much more than you can even imagine. You are made in his image, and the more you display all he has placed within you, the more you bring him glory. And when we bring him glory, we feel joy, freedom, and purpose. Life becomes a gift rather than a chore.

Will you believe that God does have a Promised Land for you? I know that you will, that you do. You are not a grumbler. You are not a doubter. You are not someone who settles for safety. You, dear reader, are a Joshua or Caleb standing on the edge of the Promised Land, seeing all that is good and saying, "Yes, this is possible!" (see Num. 13). Then you take the steps of faith, fight the battles, and go the distance to take possession of all God has for you.

Spend your life being fully alive.

Then spend eternity full of joy.

When God said his plans for you are good, he meant it.

Because Regret Hurts More Than Risk

Imagine you step onto the porch of a retirement home. A few contented residents sit in the sunshine enjoying a peaceful day. You decide to spend some time talking with each one. You ask about their childhoods, their families, and what has mattered most in their lives. Then you ask a single question: What do you regret most? The answers startle you. One by one they share not about epic mistakes, business failures, or family falling-outs. They tell you about what they *didn't do*.

Does that sound far-fetched? As I mentioned earlier in this book, studies have been done asking older people what they regret most about their lives. The overwhelming answer: what they didn't do is much more painful than what they did. It seems that even when you try and fail, you walk away with something, even if it's just a lesson learned that can be applied next time. But if you don't give it a shot at all, you're guaranteed to end up with nothing.

Our brains are wired with what scientists like to call a "negativity bias." It has many different facets, but long story short, it means we pay more attention to the negative. When we're thinking through taking a risk or pursuing a dream, our mind has no trouble summoning up every worst-case scenario imaginable. I believe God gave us this ability to navigate life, to survive, and to make overall sound decisions. But when it comes to our dreams, this normally handy feature of who we are can get in the way.

There's a time and place for your negativity bias to serve you, but it's not when God has just asked you to take a leap of faith. The wonderfully made systems in our minds are much like the computer I'm typing on right now. I'm very thankful the software is there, but I know it's up to me to apply it and even override it when necessary. We've talked about overcoming fear, and that's exactly what we've got to do if we're going to be one of the residents sitting on the front porch of the retirement home telling stories of victory and not tales of regret.

We have one life to live. We have one shot at fulfilling the purpose God has for us. And while we live in a culture that values safety to the extreme, I don't see God doing the same thing. Throughout Scripture he places people in precarious situations and then comes through in miraculous ways. But there is always that moment when they must decide, "Will I choose obedience over safety?" Yes, God promises us security, but safety and comfort are another matter.

Safety is ultimately an illusion, a grasp for control that makes our minds calm down. But none of us are truly safe. A meteor could crash through my ceiling right now, and that would be the end of me in this life. The idea that we can be safe can trick us into avoiding risks that God is asking us to take. And ironically, when we risk with him it's the safest thing we can do. Because he gives us what truly can't be taken away—security. Security doesn't depend on external circumstances. It's invincible. So you may be taking more risks than ever before and feeling more fear than you think you can stand. But actually you're more secure than when you felt safe because you're right in the middle of God's plan.

Your brain will rebel against this idea. It will tell you that survival is paramount (whether that survival is physical or just emotional and social). It will tell you that if you take that step, reach out to that person, push past that limit, your world will come to an end. That's your brain's job, at least the amygdala, which is where the flight or fight response resides. But another part of you (your prefrontal cortex—the reasoning part of your mind) can respond with, "Thank you for looking out for me, amygdala. I'm glad you showed me there could be danger here. And you're right—but the greatest danger of all is missing what God has for me. I serve a limitless God for whom all things are possible, so I'm moving ahead with him."

If you move ahead and nothing works out as you planned, you still have what matters most. And that's knowing you were faithful. Your role is obedience. God's role is results. That's the only way to live without regret. As John Piper explains:

> This is the promise that empowers us to take risks for the sake of Christ. It is not the impulse of heroism, or

> the lust for adventure, or the courage of self-reliance, or the need to earn God's favor. It is simple trust in Christ—that in him God will do everything necessary so that we can enjoy making much of him forever. Every good poised to bless us, and every evil arrayed against us, will in the end help us boast only in the cross, magnify Christ, and glorify our Creator. Faith in these promises frees us to risk and to find in our own experience that it is better to lose our life than to waste it.[13]

Before you get to sit on a front porch and talk about your life one day, make sure you live in a way that lets you tell stories of God's glory that will knock everyone else off their rockers.

Because It's Really Not about You

As Rick Warren's infamous line at the beginning of *The Purpose Driven Life* declares, "It's not about you." We read those words with a giggle, a bit of shock, a twinge of guilt. Because really our biggest battle in life is exactly that: not making it about us.

Even our God-sized dreams can become about us. When that happens, the enemy will try to tell you to stop. He'll whisper that you shouldn't be doing this at all, because really it's all about you. Swat that thought away like you would a stray fly buzzing in your ear. You are human, and you will never be able to pursue a worthwhile goal without it being about you at times. The point is not to say, "This isn't about me at all" but instead to say, "This isn't all about me." Of course God wants part of the dream to be about you. The entire story of the gospel is about partnership, intimacy, relationship. The best loves, the best marriages, are not one-sided. They have give-and-take, shared joys, two hearts coming together in a way that benefits them both.

It's the same with the journey we share with Jesus. He wants us to be part of the dreams he's placed within us. What we're to guard against is simply the temptation to put ourselves first, to make our dream an idol, to forget the Giver and cling to the gift.

Feeling guilty? Don't—that's not what this is about. We all face those temptations. Even Jesus did in his face-off with the enemy in the wilderness. Simply realize that they're part of the journey and you will have to address them at some point.

So if it's really not about us, then what is it all about? The answer actually is not "what" but instead "who." Because when it comes down to it, all of our lives, all we do, are simply to be about making much of Jesus. As John the Baptist said, "He must increase, but I must decrease" (John 3:30 KJV). Your dream is a gift God gives to you. What you make of it is your gift to him. You have an opportunity to bring glory and honor to the God who hung the stars in place. Isn't that amazing? He could do anything with just a breath, just a word, and yet instead he chooses to partner with you.

It's all about God.

It's all about his kingdom, his purposes, his name, his plans that stretch throughout eternity. We're all part of a much bigger story. We're invited to play a role in the only real truth. It's an incredible honor.

What does that say about you? It says that you are chosen. You are treasured. You are cherished. You are important to God's work in this generation. It means he has entrusted you with something very meaningful, a piece of his heart reflected in yours.

You are made in the image of God, and there is a part of who he is that will only get expressed through who you are. None of us can possibly contain all of who he is—only Jesus could do that—but who you are reveals a tiny bit of who he is in a way no one else ever will.

Your God-sized dreams are not just about making his purposes and plans a reality. They are also about revealing his character through you. Who you are on this journey is just as important as what you do.

It's a paradox. A mystery. It's not about you, and yet you are right there in the middle of it. Think of yourself as a lightbulb. You're there to shine, and yet really what matters most is simply what you illuminate, what you allow others to see.

The God of the universe has chosen you as his ambassador, his partner, his way of sharing his light with the world. You may not feel qualified. You may not feel ready. You may not think you can do what he asks. Listen, my friend: you are all you need to be to do all he's called you to do. "It's not about you" can be hard words to hear, but in this context they can also bring a profound sense of relief. You do not have to be superwoman to make God's plans happen in your life. Because it's ultimately about him, and your role is simply to let his light flow through you. You're the vessel—he's the source.

I'm smiling as I write these words and think of you. Maybe you're in an office. Perhaps you're curled up on a couch. You could be on a plane or tucked under the covers with sleep coming soon.

Go ahead and shine, my friend.

"But that's not humble."

"I don't want it to be about me."

When I talk to women about living the purpose and calling God has for their lives, I hear those two phrases often (and I've said them myself).

And yet . . .

> You are the light of the world. A town built on a hill cannot be hidden. Neither do people light a lamp and put it under a bowl. Instead they put it on its stand, and it gives

> light to everyone in the house. In the same way, let your light shine before others, that they may see your good deeds and glorify your Father in heaven. (Matt. 5:14–16)

In other words, let what you do shine in a way that helps people see who God is.

Yes, people will see you.

That's okay.

You're still being humble.

And it's certainly not about you.

We all know a lightbulb isn't ever the main attraction—it just enables us to see what matters most. So go ahead and shine, my friend. Brighter than ever.

Oh yes, that's beautiful!

I think I can see the glow all the way from here.

Keep it up, friend. Keep making much of the One who made you. You bring so much light to the world and so much joy to his heart when you do.

Final Thoughts

I'm wishing we were together right now. By now we wouldn't just meet at a coffee shop. We'd hang out at my house. I'd pull up a chair for you at my kitchen table. I'd pour you a cup of something warm and cozy. Then I'd raise my mug high in the air and propose a toast: to you, to your dream, and most of all to the God who gave it to you. As our mugs clinked and we sipped, we'd talk of how this journey is going for you. You could tell me about your victories and I'd cheer with you. You could tell me about the hard parts too. Then I'd do the same.

By the time we got to our last drop, I imagine we would both be ready to say the same thing: "It's worth it."

It always is in the end. There will be days in your dream when the fog of fear or doubt descends and you forget. It's okay—the sun will come out again and you will remember. There will be times when you're tired and you just want to stop, but somehow you'll find the strength to keep going. There will be moments when it seems nothing is coming together, and then God will show up and split your Red Sea, and you'll watch in amazement at what he can do.

It's a wild ride, this dreaming. Our role is simply to hang on with all our hearts. And to remember that it's worth it because God is worth it. The One who called us by name, took our place on the cross, fashioned our hearts, and walks with us every day is the ultimate reward. He's the reason we keep going, keep pressing on, and refuse to give up.

As we sat at the table, there would be an empty chair across from us. I'd tell you of how as a little girl I used to have my mom pull up an extra chair for Jesus. We'd both laugh at my innocence. I'd tell you that sometimes it almost seemed as if I could see him sitting across the table, smiling, enjoying our conversation.

And in moments like these, as we talk of dreams and the Giver of them, it still feels that way too.

Go Deeper Guide

(Download a printable version with lines for writing at www.holley gerth.com on the "Books & More" page.)

1. God doesn't have a plan B for you. How does knowing that affect your perception of how much your life matters?
2. When do you feel closest to God as you're pursuing your dream?
3. When do you feel most alive and fulfilled?
4. Regret hurts more than risk. What do you think of that statement?
5. "It's not about you." What helps you get beyond yourself and focus on God's kingdom in your life and dreams?
6. What else makes your God-sized dream worth it?
7. If you don't pursue your God-sized dream, who will it affect? If you do pursue it, who will that affect?

Dream It. Do It.

Review what you've written in the chapters before this one. What's different than when you started? Take a few moments to thank God for where he's brought you so far and where you're going in the future.

10

God-Sized Dreams **Stories**

We tend to think God-sized dreams happen through larger-than-life people. The stuff of legends. The ones who seem to dwell on unreachable pedestals. But that's a myth. God-sized dreams always happen through ordinary folks. People like you, me, and your neighbor across the street.

The stories that follow are about real God-sized dreamers. You might bump into them at the grocery store. You might sit across the aisle from them at church. You might read their blog or be friends with them on Facebook.

None of them would describe themselves as exceptionally brave or outrageously adventurous. But they're all consistently, lovingly living in an obedient way that makes a difference.

I've learned a lot from their stories, and I hope you will too.

One disclaimer: when we read the God-sized dream stories of others, it's always tempting to compare. Please resist that urge. As we've talked about all along the way, the God-sized dream he has for you perfectly fits the size of your heart. *There is only one you.*

What I want you to see in these stories isn't "how to" but instead more of the heart of what it means to be a God-sized dreamer. I imagine I could include your story here too. And who knows? Maybe someday I will.

By the way, these are all women I know in real life. They're not stories from the internet or out of a magazine listing the world's most influential people. They're women I love, celebrate, and have the privilege of cheering on as they pursue their dreams. I tell their stories the same way I would share them with you over a cup of coffee. Because you know by now that's just how we do things around here.

While You're Waiting: Kristen Strong

In fifth grade Kristen chose staying in to do schoolwork before going out to recess. She worked hard and slept little even in high school because she was bent on giving maximum effort so she could shine.

If effort alone could have brought ultimate success in high school and beyond, she would have graduated valedictorian. She did well but was still not the "A" girl she desperately wanted to be. She says, "No matter what I did—or how much effort I expended—I fell into that expansive middle labeled 'average.'"

She shared with me how she couldn't enjoy what small victories she had because her good was never good enough. She thought God worked through and was most proud of those whose life's work and worth were labeled with a big, tangible A. Something everyone could see for themselves. The grade A end result proved their God-sized dreams were realized.

Kristen says that early attitude carried right on into her grown-up years too. "Unfortunately, I have bought into this for part of my adult life too. That the visible results—what I can see right now—determine the success of my God-sized dream."

But then Kristen began discovering that's not how God works. She says, "His God-sized dream in me is taking something I have little patience for . . . time. Like a fitful toddler, I want what I want and I want it now. But God says, 'Listen, girl. I planted this dream in you. Since I planted it, I get to say how long it takes to grow and how tall it's going to be. I'm working on you more through this dream than you realize.' "

Kristen adds that she now knows God first pushed her to work hard as a young girl because it would lay a foundation for going the distance and appreciating a slower path instead of a quick sprint to her dreams. So she's shifting her thinking to look at the journey as what matters most rather than the destination. Kristen says on the journey we can:

- ***Build relationships.*** Ever try to carry on a conversation while sprinting down a track? It's kinda hard. While slower times of life can be frustrating, they can also be opportunities for meeting folks and nurturing relationships.
- ***Improve our skills.*** If we want to learn and improve our craft, we need to take the time to study hard so we can learn what God wants us to learn.
- ***Fellowship with God.*** We want to enjoy his very real and active presence. We will grow and flourish most when we are in regular communication with the One who instilled our dreams in the first place.

Sometimes God-sized dreams seem so powerful we could burst from the excitement and scariness of it all. If God is working on us through the journey and not just the destination, we want to give him some serious glory in the process. Kristen sums it up this way: "I want to get caught up in him rather than results." It's about each step with God along the way and throughout eternity.

> *You make known to me the path of life;*
> *you will fill me with joy in your presence,*
> *with eternal pleasures at your right hand.* (Ps. 16:11)

And you know what else? When God instills a God-sized dream in your heart, he is telling you, "You are enough." You know enough. You have what it takes. You may not think it, feel it, or see anything in front of you that proves it, but it's true nonetheless. Sometimes it may take missing-recess, up-all-night kind of effort, but keep going the distance.

God-sized dreams penetrate deep. So if it seems yours is taking time to bloom, perhaps it means he is still growing it. Don't give up on the fact that his dream for you (and the wait!) is ripe with purpose.

Over the last few years, I've watched Kristen continue to be faithful when it comes to waiting for God's plans in her life. Right now her family is in the midst of waiting to hear if her husband will be deployed to active military duty again. Her dream is for all of them to be a family in one place, but she knows God may have other plans.

Kristen and her husband also recently discovered their young daughter will need surgery to correct a genetic feature in her spine. Another God-sized dream for Kristen is a completely healthy daughter, but it seems there will be some medical hills to climb before that's a reality. As she shared the news with her friends and family on her blog, *Chasing Blue Skies* (www.chasingblueskies.net), Kristen wrote:

> The Lord is always revealing and saving and proclaiming. Sometimes this fact shows up in jump up and down good news, like twin lines on a pregnancy test. Sometimes it shows up real quiet, like on a difficult but certain x-ray. Either way, it shows up because *he* shows up. He doesn't reveal and then take a nap or proclaim and then forget about us. He moves and acts always, even during those dreaded ambiguous uncertain times. Especially then.
>
> Every bit of bad news holds good news because He. Is. Always. Good.[14]

In the good, the bad, and the in-between times, Kristen has learned that God-sized dreams are not about our circumstances but instead about the One who holds our lives in his hands.

I love this beautiful, openhearted God-sized dreamer who lights up the room with her smile and knows how to make anyone's day brighter even if she's having a difficult one of her own. Kristen isn't just waiting—she's thriving. She's daily living by grace as she trades her "not good enough" striving for a "more than enough" God who loves her deeply and shows us all more about how to do the same.

When You Have More Than One God-Sized Dream: Heather Steck

We got married one day apart. We had the same flippy blonde hair. We could sing along to every Amy Grant song. We also both worked at DaySpring, the Christian subsidiary of Hallmark. I wrote cards and Heather made them beautiful with her stunning designs. We ate lunch together, played fun games with our husbands on the weekends, and even shopped at the same stores. I'd never met someone whose heart and life seemed so parallel to mine.

We both talked of having kids one day. My husband and I began that journey first, and seven years later it seems God has called us to focus in other places right now. Heather and Tony quickly became pregnant with their first son, Micah. The day she told me we both hugged each other and expressed joy as well as the sadness of not sharing that experience. It seemed God had different plans for each of us in the next season ahead.

Heather gave me the gift of watching someone become a mother—a wonderful, loving, creative mother. She gave me another gift too. She let me watch her wrestle with what the changes in her life meant for her God-sized dreams.

Heather didn't ever think of herself as a "stay-at-home" mom. She respected and admired women who made that choice. Yet it was clear she had an incredible gift when it came to designing and God had called her to DaySpring. Still, as Micah grew and a daughter, Lily, arrived as well, it seemed she heard a new call too.

She sensed God whispering that for this season, he wanted her to be able to focus more on being a mom. We talked about that transition many times over lunch. Heather wrestled with it intensely. Even when she made the transition, she confessed that it was much harder than she imagined, although it was what a part of her deep inside really wanted too.

She had two God-sized dreams that seemed to be in conflict with each other. Heather says:

> It took some time to adjust to the idea. Those first few months were very hard. Then one day a quote stuck out to me. It said, "You can have it all—but you can't have it

> all at once." That changed my perspective. I began to think of my dreams in terms of seasons. For now, I knew that the God-sized dream of being home with my kids was supposed to be my main focus. That was a dream that didn't come naturally to me. My other dream, of fulfilling my creative calling, had always been there, and now it seemed I needed to pursue it differently. For a while I stepped away completely from that dream but then gradually began doing freelance work and finding other ways to express that desire of my heart. In a few years, both of my kids will be in school and my God-sized dreams will change again. I used to think that dreams stayed the same all of our lives. Now I understand that they change right along with us and what God has in each season.

I know many other women like Heather. Some have felt called to be at home like she did. Others sensed God prompting them to continue working. Many have found hybrids of both that fit their families in unique ways.

During the time when Heather and I talked a lot about our dreams and her decision, I came across a quote that I loved. Jill Churchill said, "There is no way to be a perfect mother and a million ways to be a good one."[15] I shared it with Heather, and we talked about those words often. Even without kids, I applied it in other ways to my life. ("There's no way to be a perfect wife, friend, writer . . . but a million ways to be a good one.")

It became our little mantra for a few years, and I still think of it from time to time. It's true of God-sized dreams as well. *There's no way to do your God-sized dream perfectly, but there are a million ways to do it well.* Our lives shift and change. Seasons come and go. Our dreams do too. But through it all one thing remains steady: the God who put those dreams within our hearts in the first place.

I'm so proud of Heather because she's a woman who listens to Jesus. She loves him with all her heart. She does whatever is in front of her with creativity and excellence, whether that's being a mom, designing something beautiful, or loving on me as her friend.

Heather is a God-sized dreamer, and she's taught me so much about faith, flexibility, and being willing to let go so God can give me even more.

Do It Afraid:
Keri Lynn

Keri remembers the first time she had to perform in freshman drama class. And every time she does, she also recalls exactly how she came to be in that freshman drama class.

It was the end of her eighth-grade year, and the counselors were explaining that in high school, students were required to take one semester of either speech or drama. Keri says, "Both options made me want to lose my lunch."

She describes herself as the quiet, shy, awkward kid who did everything in her power to avoid the spotlight. Simply being called on in class to answer a question made her break into an instant cold sweat. And now, sitting in the cafeteria, she had just been informed that she would have to spend an entire semester taking a class that would require her to stand up and speak out. Yikes!

Keri decided to take speech, not because she wanted to but because it was the lesser of two evils. But her best friend had other plans. Her friend had heard a rumor that there was only one freshman drama class and concluded that it was the only way to guarantee the two of them would have a class together. "So I caved to peer pressure," Keri confesses.

The following September Keri found herself standing on a stage with twenty teenagers and one teacher watching her. She was supposed to perform. Looking back on that moment, Keri exclaims, "I don't remember what I had to do. All I remember was the absolute terror that gripped my heart!"

Keri remembers telling her teacher she was afraid. His response? "Do it afraid!" He told her fear was good; it would heighten her senses and give her a rush of adrenaline that would help her performance.

Keri says, "I promise you it didn't help. It was awful! The only consolation was that I made it to the ladies' room before losing my lunch. But over the weeks something strange began to happen. I started looking forward to my drama class. I even started feeling excited when it was my turn to perform. Don't get me wrong, I was still scared every time I faced the stairs leading to the stage, but I was learning to manage my fears."

Keri wound up taking four full years of drama. She joined the competitive drama squad and traveled all over the state competing and winning awards, thank you very much. And she loved it!

Years later, Keri reflects on that turning point in her life:

> I still love the stage. In fact, I get paid to be onstage—well, it's actually a studio, not a stage. But there is a microphone, and there are people watching (listening). Friends ask me how I can do it. They ask if it's scary to be on the radio as a morning show host for KLRC every day. But for me, honestly, it's not scary. Not now. Because I pushed past the fear. I learned to overcome my anxiety.
>
> Here's the problem with following Jesus. Every time I find myself relaxing . . . I find myself stirred. Every time I think I've arrived . . . I realize that I have further to go. You see, God won't let me quit dreaming. And

> the dreams just get bigger and scarier. To tell you the truth, it makes me want to run for the hills!
>
> But I can't. The pull to be with him is just too strong. And over and over I hear him whispering, "Do it afraid! Push past the fear! Overcome the anxiety! I'm here. I'll hold your hand. I will catch you if you fall."
>
> I want to settle in and rest here, in this place of comfort. I want to be content. But God isn't calling us to settle; he's calling us to follow.

Follow him into unchartered territory.
Follow him into new relationships.
Follow him into taking risks and chasing dreams.
As Keri learned, he's calling all of us to "Do it afraid!"

Permission to Have Joy along the Way: Bonnie Gray

Bonnie has depended on God since her early years as the oldest girl growing up in a single-parent family with little means. God was the only daddy she knew, so she stuck to him for dear life.

Dysfunctional upbringing? Bonnie sucked up the words of Jesus like they were the last oxygen mask left in a broken plane crashing down.

Dreams of becoming a writer dashed for a practical engineering degree? Bonnie chose to find her joy in serving others instead.

A traumatic stint in missions left Bonnie with years marked by solitude and prayer, while singleness past thirty handed her questions about the gift of singleness.

Even though Bonnie later got the surprising joy of getting married, she's been learning to be content with the story line of her life for a very long time. She got so good at living with the disappointment of yesterday that she had trouble opening up her heart to taste joy in today. Bonnie shares:

> I'd say I'm a happy person who loves to laugh, eat chocolate, and enjoy friends. And I can't describe the thrill my heart feels when I get to encourage others.
>
> As for personal joy, the kind that is God-sized? I like to stick to the kind of joy that comes out of suffering and trials. Not because I'm all that spiritual. That's just the kind I know about.
>
> I'm comfortable with walking through deserts. I'm used to wearing sandals and getting sand between my toes. Trouble is, I was walking along fine until one day I stepped out of the desert and into new waters of healing. Scenes in my life that previously looked void of purpose took on a new shape, color, and sound. I started seeing God in the background.
>
> I realized as hard and painful as my losses have been, Jesus's love for me grew deeper in spite of it all.

Bonnie describes always feeling like an ugly duckling with experiences she wishes had never been written into her life. But since Jesus started showing her how he carried her through it all, she now sees the fruits of love, faithfulness, and gentleness that he's planted in her, along with each sorrow.

She explains, "A new kind of joy has been growing in my heart. It's a growing desire for beauty even though I've experienced the barrenness of dreams. This joy is calling me to embrace abundance and celebrate the opportunities he's placed in my life. Like a new pair of shoes, this joy is very uncomfortable. This joy doesn't feel like it's me. I'm afraid to lean into this joy because maybe it won't last."

Questions Bonnie never asked before are now challenging this new freedom.

How will this joy change me?

Will my friends like this new me?

If I embrace this joy, will I love feeling this way more than depending on God?

Ultimately, all this awkwardness is a question about trusting in God's love.

Bonnie describes the permission she's found to have joy in her God-sized dreams with these words: "I'm used to snuggling in Jesus's arms. Now he wants me to ride on his shoulders. Do I really deserve to be here? God is saying, 'Yes, you deserve to be here. Because I love you.'"

Bonnie continues to write about her journey on www.faithbarista.com. She's moving forward with joy, hope, and the promise of growing into all God has created her to be and everything he has for her to do.

When Your Dreams Are Bigger Than You Are: Kristen Welch

The house was quiet. Kristen's family had been asleep for hours. The night was still, but her thoughts weren't. Kristen says, "I knew if I closed my eyes, I would see her face again."

Kristen never thought of herself as a dreamer. She shares, "*I'm a realist,* I would say to the gleam in my hubby's eye, the one he'd get right after he shared one of his big ideas. I like my feet on the ground. I like to know the beginning and the end. I like safe things."

After returning from a trip to Africa in March with Compassion International, Kristen knew she was being called to a God-sized dream. She was able to push it off during her busy day, hectic with kids, but at night all the suppressed thoughts would surface in her dreams.

The girl was there, feet caked with mud, her eyes distant. Hollow. She was desperately searching for something.

It was hope. And she had none.

When God began dropping the dream of The Mercy House into Kristen's heart and connecting the dots—hers with others who had the same recurring dream—she wanted to run.

She describes that season: "I kept saying, 'It's too big. This is too big for me.' (What I was really saying? 'God, I'm scared. This isn't safe. I can't.') But then I was reminded by this anonymous quote: 'God gives us dreams a size too big so that we can grow into them.'"

God wants us to stretch, to reach beyond ourselves and our own capabilities. It's there that we grow into our God-sized dreams.

Kristen feels clothed in a dream a size too big. She has more questions than answers, more fear than courage. But she has asked him what he required of her, and he answered:

> *He has shown you, O mortal, what is good.*
> *And what does the Lord require of you?*
> *To act justly and to love mercy*
> *and to walk humbly with your God. (Mic. 6:8)*

Does your dream feel too big for you? It probably is. But God is bigger.

Now when Kristen sees the girl's face in her dream, she doesn't turn away.

Because hope is on its way.

Kristen launched The Mercy House, which exists to provide alternative options for pregnant girls living in the streets of Kenya. The Mercy House aids them in nutrition, housing, prenatal care, counseling, biblical teaching, and job skills for sustainable living. Find out more at www.mercyhousekenya.org.

Building Dreams: Angie Washington

Much like Kristen's, this is a dream come true story for those in need.

Busy streets in a faraway place make it easy to overlook little ones in need. But one day a pair of feet pause and eyes look down to see the children—the ones who curl into their tiny spots on earth. The crowds continue to rush by, but change is coming.

"Somebody needs to do something about the orphans in our city," whispers a Voice.

"Yes, they do" is whispered back with a shake of the head and a shrug as footsteps hurry away. It's hard to embrace the need.

But for three more days this scene and conversation repeat.

"Somebody should do something about the orphans in our city," says Someone persistent, insistent.

The response slowly changes: "Yes, we may not be able to help them all, but we can help some."

Angie's husband listened to Someone, the One, and they started the House of Dreams Orphanage in Cochabamba, Bolivia. This dream began with months of paper trails. Finally a building could be prepared. Staff were hired. Beds waited. Warm clothes and healthy meals sat ready. This House of Dreams would be filled with dreamers, children who needed Someone to be their Father. Children whose flickering hope could be stoked and set ablaze once again.

That was over four years ago.

Now learn from Angie's little dreamers how to dream. She says:

> First, they dream with eyes closed. The pavement they sit on is cold, the scorn on the faces that pass by too harsh. Starving, they lift a weak hand to the air and beg

> for help. Heads bow to the ground. They close their eyes and paint beauty in the darkness.
>
> Slowly they begin to dream with their eyes open. They are brought in from the frigid night to safety. They are fed and clothed. Their dreams are coming true. They know the tangible love of Someone real. But wait—that is not the end.
>
> Their eyes open wide, they look around and dream through the eyes of those around us. The goodness that was poured on them, they pour on others. Hands that once reached out begging now reach out healing. The extended arms of Someone made our dreams come true; we follow him. Our arms stretch out in sacrifice and love.

Are you dreaming with your eyes squeezed tight shut today? Don't lose hope. You are not alone.

Maybe your eyes are adjusting to the light of his goodness, of dreams come true. We celebrate with you today!

To those living a dream life, might we invite you to see through the eyes of those around you? You may be a dream come true as you follow the nudge of Someone close.

"Freely you have received; freely give" (Matt. 10:8).

Angie and her husband started the House of Dreams in Bolivia. You can find out more at www.houseofdreamsorphanage.com.

The Art of Dreaming: Dee Kasberger

Right away Dee exclaims, "Red Letter Words is a God-sized dream. There is no possible conceivable way that I could have planned for it to become what it is."

What Red Letter Words is today started as a thought, an idea for Scripture as art, big and plain for everyone to see. Bold and readable across the room. The focal point of a living room. That was 2003. It was a desire of Dee's heart.

Except that the timing was off. It wasn't the right season. Ecclesiastes 3 says that there is a time for everything. And 2003 was busy. Dee says:

> I was too busy doing too many things and not doing any of them very well. We had three young kids, and I was working for my husband, who at the time had two companies, a photography studio and a digital printing lab. I was volunteering at school and at church and at soccer. Whatever spare time I had was spent at the mall or reading gossip magazines. (Now, I am not saying that I don't still enjoy shopping as much as the next girl, but when I was on a first-name basis with every store manager, that was not good.) My worth was tied up in what I was doing.

Fast-forward a few years and Dee is home with their fourth baby. Her husband has sold his photography studio, and she is no longer working for Color, Inc.

They had decided that enough was enough. So Dee stopped working and volunteering so much and concentrated on staying home, raising the kids, and managing the house. Dee describes that season:

> I never thought that I would be so content with the ordinary daily cleaning and laundry and groceries and everything involved with keeping a home.
>
> I decided to seek first his kingdom.
>
> God's way of doing things.

> I had always done things my way. But when I sought after his kingdom, I became more and more aware of exactly who I was in Christ.
>
> A sinner saved by grace.
>
> Created in his image.
>
> Blessed and highly favored.
>
> Worthy. Redeemed. Loved.
>
> I was content and happy. And it wasn't until I was content with the ordinary that God opened the door to the extraordinary.

Dee started having small blocks of time during the day that she was so thankful for—spare quiet moments to work on her dream of Scripture as art. Because she had long before decided that whatever spare time she was given was going to be used to bring God glory.

The ideas for Red Letter Words became clearer. The art would look like an erased chalkboard. With big text. With Scripture that had personal meaning to her. After much trial and error, Dee made pieces for her house and started giving them to friends and family members for Christmas and birthdays and baby showers and wedding presents.

In 2008 Dee started an Etsy store. She wrote down the vision. Every month it was the same: "Bring God's glory to lots of people." It is still the same vision, and www.redletterwords.com soon followed. Dee says:

> It is so exciting to see what God's plan is for Red Letter Words. His plan is always for good, and I love walking by the foyer and reading Jeremiah 29:11. Over the years I have held on to and confessed out loud many Scriptures at different seasons of life . . . most of which have been made into Red Letter Words prints.
>
> God is no respecter of persons . . . this is for you too—

> You were created in his image.
> You are blessed and highly favored.
> Worthy. Redeemed. Loved.

God is endlessly creative in the dreams he gives us—and the unexpected ways he makes them come true in our lives!

It's Not Too Late: Mela Kamin

Mela always wanted to be an artist—but singer was someone else's dream.

She was a jock, then a journalist, and then a juice-slingin' mom of three. Sure, she sang—but with the radio and to her kids (easy crowd).

She searched for an activity to pour herself into. Not that she wasn't already busy, but she was looking for "her" something.

Mela wondered, *Whatever happened to the creative, dazzling, big dreamer? What became of the girl who graduated in three and a half years, gave the commencement speech about being an "agent of change," and soared into an exciting career?*

She says, "It turns out she was afraid—afraid, after spending years at home trying to be everything to everyone, that she was gone for good. Afraid she was too old or too ordinary to do anything worthwhile. But a singer . . . really?"

Two years ago, as a middle-aged mom living in the suburbs of Minnesota, Mela was a far cry from the picture of most recording artists. She had no musical training, fan base, or blog readership to support an album. Some people closest to her didn't even know Mela could sing.

God-sized dreams, though, aren't easy, expected, or practical.

No matter her stage of life or missing credentials, what she had far outweighed what she lacked.

She had Holy Spirit power from a God who says that with him, *all* things are possible.

She had a deep-down desire to use her gifts in a bolder way.

And she had just enough gumption to go for it, even faced with Goliath-size fear.

Just call her David.

David wasn't the first (or fifth) choice or the most qualified to fight. When he stood up, *no one* saw it coming. He was unlikely *and* unqualified.

Mela knew her fears could have counted her out. She felt the enemy telling her to keep her head down, go through the motions, and keep her mouth shut.

But as she pushed through, God's plans, and the faith he provides, kicked in. People, events, and songs were placed in her life, on her lap and on her lips.

Mela explains, "I couldn't ignore it any more than David could ignore his call to action. He won, knowing God gave him everything he needed . . . not by being the biggest or best but by being the boldest."

So what got Mela out on the battlefield?

Someone pushed her. A friend helped her put her hopes on paper, and that was the first time she shared her dream to be a singer.

Her friend didn't laugh. She told Mela it was awesome. And Mela finally saw the possibilities.

Once she started writing songs, everything she knew about herself came back into view. Passion resurfaced, confidence came bouncing back, and she couldn't stop smiling.

God had brought her back to life for such a time as this.

Then doors opened and people appeared.

Mela met musician Carl Herrgesell at a women's event, playing keys for Kathy Troccoli. Mela told her story, and as only God can orchestrate, Carl offered to produce her album.

Just. Like. That.

Two months later, Mela was in a Nashville recording studio meeting her coproducer, Dan Needham. He and Carl lovingly guided her through the process and took all the pressure off. Five trips to Nashville and four short months later, that big dream became Mela's debut album, "Summer in My Soul."

Mela exclaims with a smile, "I'm here to tell you—there are no expiration dates on your gifts or your dreams. Start where you are with what you have, and don't be surprised when God makes a way."

"Each of you should use whatever gift you have received to serve others, as faithful stewards of God's grace in its various forms" (1 Pet. 4:10).

Dreams Even in the Middle of the Desert: Ashley Wells

In the midst of the most difficult journey of her life, Ashley rediscovered God was much bigger than she had ever imagined. He was with her and carrying her through her journey. There was Someone to rescue her.

After she had felt hurt and isolation because of infertility, God, by his wonderful grace, opened Ashley's eyes to the fact that he had a plan for her and for her future. He was guiding her through.

Ashley shares, "I didn't know all of his plans for my life (and I still don't), nor do I understand why he had led me through my personal valley. However, in the midst of my journey, God

I sit in front of the computer and stare at the screen.

In this modern world of words, it seems there are so many numbers—so many ways to compare.

Facebook friends. Twitter followers. Blog subscribers.

Isn't it that way in other areas of our lives too?

Dress sizes. Paychecks. Square footage.

And sometimes we assume that those with the most or the biggest must be God's favorites.

But that's not the way it works.

Not at all.

Whatever you're created to do, God will make it happen, and you don't have to be perfect.

It's not a contest—it's a calling.

Thank you for what you do.

Thank you for being who you are.

You matter and make a difference even more than you'll ever know.

Immeasurably so.

planted a seed, a God-sized dream, that would grow in my heart and bloom."

The God-sized dream that he planted in Ashley's heart was that he was going to use her story to encourage other women in the midst of their suffering. God would use her hurt and experience to help others going through hard times too.

When Ashley first felt the reality of this God-sized dream, she pushed it aside. How could she possibly help others when she felt like she was drowning? She thought, *Lord, this just can't be true!*

She continues, "I remember when I started to feel whole again. I remember learning to trust him again. I started reading God's Word more faithfully. I developed a stronger prayer life. I started giving him my anxieties, worries, and stress. I gave him my infertility. I put it in his hands. I started to trust him no matter the outcome. I began to find healing. I felt steady again, resting in his hands."

God has been guiding Ashley beyond the valley (though still childless) for about two years. That seed, the God-sized dream, bloomed this year as she wrote about her journey and how God has led her every step.

Ashley admits, "Sharing wasn't easy. As I began to write, I felt like I was not spiritual enough, or had not experienced this trial the 'right way' (like there is a right way!), or that I had suffered too much and too deeply for good to come from sharing. Yet slowly I began rejoicing as I continued to write my story, because after I shared about my hurt, I got to share about the hope that I had found."

Even more so, Ashley is now rejoicing as women are reading her book, *How My Soul Yearns,* and finding hope in God. Hope in the midst of the valley. Hope in the midst of suffering. Hope in the midst of this sin-tainted world.

Ashley exclaims, "Only a God-sized dream can lead a hurt and wounded woman to share her story to help other hurt and wounded women! What a wonderful God we have that he uses us in these ways!"

Conclusion

God-sized dreams come in all shapes and sizes. They're not limited by geography, age, or circumstances. I could fill up thousands more pages with God-sized dreams. I hope you've enjoyed this little taste. What spoke to you most in these stories? What would you share with these women if you met them?

I'd love to hear your God-sized dream story too. You can share it with me at www.holleygerth.com.

You are part of your own beautiful story. It's being written by the Author of life, and he has more in store for you than you can even imagine. The best is yet to be for you, my friend.

Go Deeper Guide

(Download a printable version with lines for writing at www.holley gerth.com on the "Books & More" page.)

1. What are you waiting on in your life right now? Which of Kristen's tips spoke to you most?
2. Have you ever had to choose between two God-sized dreams you really wanted, like Heather? What guided you as you made that decision?
3. Keri tells us to "Do it afraid!" Describe a time in your childhood when you did so and how that impacted your life.
4. Bonnie is learning how to have joy along the path to her God-sized dreams. What have you learned about joy through your own journey?
5. Kristen's and Angie's God-sized dreams both led them to serve the poor. What's your definition of "poor"? Is it more than just financial? Who in your life can you serve?
6. Dee's dream meant expressing her creativity in a new way. What do you do to express yours? (And everyone is creative in some way—it just means the ways that God brings life into the world through you.)
7. Mela thought it might be too late for her dream. Have you ever felt that way? What's the truth instead?
8. Ashley discovered her God-sized dream in a most unlikely place—the middle of her personal desert. Have you ever found a blessing in an unexpected place or situation in your life?

— *Dream It. Do It.* —

Reading the God-sized dreams of others can encourage us in our own as well. Choose a biography, memoir, or blog of someone you admire, and spend some time reading their story this week. Perhaps the best one of all is the story of Joshua and Caleb in the Old Testament book of Numbers.

11

Commissioning **You**

The room pulsed with energy. In every corner you could hear the sounds of excitement. Over one hundred women had gathered in this place. As I stepped onto the stage, I could see smiling faces looking back at me. Each of these women had her own business as a Blessings Unlimited consultant. Each one represented a God-sized dream come true.

I could see faces of all ages and shades in the audience. Some were single, others grandmothers. From every stage and walk of life, they were here because passion for their faith and connecting with other women bound them together.

I imagine if I could see all of the readers of this book in one room, it might feel the same way. Perhaps you're reading this page on a plane, from the corner of your couch, or on the screen of an e-reader as you sit in a local park. If you look around right now, you might not even see anyone else near you.

But you, my sister, are not alone.

We are never alone in our God-sized dreams.

At the end of the session with the Blessings Unlimited women, I asked them to stand up. I commissioned them to go out into the world, to live the dreams within their hearts, to make a difference in a new and powerful way wherever they were called to be.

And I want to do the same for you.

You Are Chosen

Before your dream ever came into being, God called your name. He formed you with love in your mother's womb and intricately designed every part of who you would become. You truly are fearfully and wonderfully made—a masterpiece by the same God who spread the oceans farther than we can even see. He numbers every hair on your head. He knows every care in your heart. You belong to him.

Your journey on this path is not by coincidence. You are here because God looked out over all of history and chose you for a particular time and purpose. You could have entered the world a hundred years ago or a thousand years from now. But you are in this generation, this time, and there will never be another you or another opportunity to do what only you are chosen to complete.

Go out there in boldness knowing that you don't have to be like anyone else. You don't have to do what any other person has done. You are chosen for one life—yours.

And the wonderful news? Whatever God chooses you to do, he will equip you for. Being chosen means you will be given all you need. Being chosen means that success simply consists of obedience and God will do the rest. Being chosen means that you have a great big God as your partner every step of the way.

I remember standing on the sidelines at recess as we lined up for an impromptu game of softball. You could see on the face of every kid in that field two words: "Pick me!" We all want to be part of something greater than ourselves. We all want to know we have something to contribute. We all want to be chosen for the team.

God looks at you and says, "I pick you." And he does so with great joy.

Dare to live as someone who knows who they belong to forever.

You Are Called

When our names are called on the playground as children, we become part of a team. We have been chosen. Yet as the game begins, it's likely that at some point we'll be given a specific position. Mine always seemed to end up being picking daisies in the outfield where no ball ever made it. But in the kingdom, there aren't any wasted positions.

You're here on earth for far more than just to take up space. God doesn't want you to just "survive" until you get home to heaven where life truly begins. When we know him, eternity begins *now*. Your days are significant, and he has no intention of wasting them. We've often relegated the word *calling* to specifically spiritual vocations like being a pastor. But the reality is, we all have unique tasks we're asked to do throughout our lives.

This means that what you do every day matters. Your life has significance. God describes himself as "I am." I love that because it's present tense. It's right here and now. If God is always with us, then there are no ordinary moments in our lives. Wherever you are right now, you are standing on holy ground.

We feel a longing for "more" in our lives because God's calling always pulls us upward and onward. He doesn't let us get complacent or too comfortable. He wants to offer us new adventures with him. Yes, we are to be content. But that's very different than being passive.

As I write this, my cell phone is sitting next to me. It will ring today. It will ring again tomorrow. Being called is an ongoing process that we live out in different ways until we get home to heaven.

Your God-sized dream is an important part of the call on your life, but it's not *the* call. The ultimate calling for all of us is an intimate relationship with Jesus. It's not about the cell phone—it's about who's on the other end of the line. It's about who's saying your name in the middle of the game and asking you to take your place.

Your life matters. You have significance. You are called.

You Are Already on Your Way

Sometimes it can seem as if we're sitting by the phone and simply waiting, wondering when God will remember us and decide to give us something important to do. But that's not the way it works. God has *already* called you. You are *already* on your way to all he has for you.

You may think, "But I've taken so many detours" or "It's too late." We tend to picture God's will like a very straight line, and if we veer off at all, then we'll never get to the destination. But God can get us there in a thousand different ways. My car has a GPS system, and its favorite phrase to say to me is "recalculating." It doesn't say, "You made a wrong turn. Cancel your trip and go home." God doesn't say that to us either. He's able to "recalculate" as many times as needed to get us where he wants us in the end.

Start where you are right now. In this very moment. On this very page. Whatever has been holding you back from your God-sized dreams, drop it on the side of the road. Tell God you're ready to move forward, and he will take care of the rest. Nothing can stand in his way—or in yours when you're following him.

You Are Needed

All it takes is a few clicks through the internet and I wind up feeling inadequate. It seems everyone is off changing the world in some distant place. There are vivid pictures, inspiring stories, and leaps of faith that make my daily journey look like a walk in the park. It's easy to silently begin to believe the words "I'm not needed."

That lie has been echoing through the church since the very beginning. Paul confronted it when he said:

> Just as a body, though one, has many parts, but all its many parts form one body, so it is with Christ. For we were all baptized by one Spirit so as to form one body—whether Jews or Gentiles, slave or free—and we were all given the one Spirit to drink. Even so the body is not made up of one part but of many.
>
> Now if the foot should say, "Because I am not a hand, I do not belong to the body," it would not for that reason stop being part of the body. And if the ear should say, "Because I am not an eye, I do not belong to the body," it would not for that reason stop being part of the body. If the whole body were an eye, where would the sense of hearing be? If the whole body were an ear, where would the sense of smell be? But in fact God has placed the parts in the body, every one of them, just as he wanted them to be. If they were all one part, where would the body be? As it is, there are many parts, but one body.
>
> The eye cannot say to the hand, "I don't need you!" And the head cannot say to the feet, "I don't need you!" (1 Cor. 12:12–21)

You are irreplaceable. What other parts of the body of Christ are doing isn't better—just different. You have something to offer that no one else can, and that's *you*.

As I type these words, I'm wearing a green rubber bracelet that arrived in the mail yesterday from my friend Jessica Turner. Engraved on the bracelet are four words: "Gitzen Girl" and "Choose Joy." Gitzen Girl, whose real name is Sara Frankl, went home to Jesus a few short weeks ago after being homebound with illness for three years even though she was only in her thirties. And yet from within her home's walls, she found a way to touch thousands of lives through her words. As she got ready to head home to Jesus, stories from all over the internet poured out, and our eyes widened as we realized how impactful Sara's life had been—even more than we knew before. Knowing Sara changed me and my definition of limitations because she turned hers into opportunities.

Sara never said, "I'm not a wife. I'm not a mom. I can't leave my house. I'm not needed." Instead she shifted her focus to others and simply asked, "Who can I encourage today?" Sara's role in the body of Christ looked different than many others', and yet she beautifully and joyfully chose to fulfill it. We can all do the same.

We need each other. I need you. You need me. None of us can do it all, but we can all do (and be) our wonderful, God-chosen part.

You Are Loved

Our culture commonly opens conversations with, "What do you do?" It's a casual question with a subtle implication—that what you do defines who you are. Yet it doesn't work that way in the kingdom. God is always first about identity and then destiny.

An odd thing can happen on the way to a God-sized dream. Somewhere along the way we can begin to confuse our dream with who we are. *You are not your dream.* Yes, it's an important part of your life and calling, but it's not your identity.

That's good news for many reasons, but perhaps this is the most encouraging of all: you are not loved for your dream. And you can't stop being loved no matter how it turns out.

Whew.

Did anyone else just breathe a sigh of relief with me?

Something within us wants a measurable way to earn love. It makes us feel more secure. We believe, "If I can just do X, then it means I must be loved." But the problem with that kind of thinking is this: as soon as we mess up, we begin to doubt that we can be loved.

You are loved as you are by a God who does not change.

Nothing you do will make him love you more.

Nothing you don't do will make him love you less.

His love for you is based on who he is and who you are as his child. Your dreams and what you accomplish in your life are part of the amazing journey you will take with God—but they are not the determiner of your relationship.

You are free to risk because you are not risking what matters most of all.

No matter what you lose, you still win in the end.

Because you'll go home with love.

You're Going to Make It

There's always this moment, this space between the knowing and the coming true. It's the hardest place. It's where most people quit.

But you're not a quitter.

God says, "This Promised Land is yours." It's *ours*. But we have to go up and possess it. And that's messy. Wild. Exhausting. It

Hello, friend, getting ready to take that next step in your day.

Through a door.

Into a dream.

On that hard path.

Wherever you are, I just want to let my words lean in close and whisper, "Keep going."

You can take the next step.

No matter how small.

Or how big.

Both make a difference.

And even if you're called to stand still, you can still keep going.

Going to your knees.

Going to the One who came for you.

You've got prayers behind you, the One who loves you beside you, and more than you can even imagine ahead of you too.

makes us think, "Maybe I didn't hear God right. Maybe I shouldn't go this way."

Go.

That's only the sound of fear whistling in your ears. You can do this. He can do this in you, through you. I've lived in that place. I know the way a heart can pound. Let's keep going, you and I, all the way to the place God promised . . . and farther up and into it for the rest of our lives.

You are not responsible for making sure you get where God wants you to go. You're simply asked to say yes when he asks you to take the next step. Much of the time you won't know where it leads. Even when you do, the purpose might be unclear. This isn't a journey about speed or efficiency. Instead it's about trust. It's about knowing and believing that the One guiding you is good.

Only God knows the way to your Promised Land. But you can lean on this: he's even more committed to getting you there than you are. Sometimes it feels as if God doesn't care about our dreams. But when they are truly from him, he's even more passionate about them than we are. He never stops bringing his purposes into being in this world.

I'm good at being a spiritual backseat driver. I like to tell God the equivalent of, "Um, I think you missed your turn." When I do, it sometimes feels as if he smiles knowingly at me, then looks back at the road and simply whispers to my heart, "Peace, daughter. I will get you there. You are free to enjoy the ride."

You are too.

Your Dream Is Going to Change the World

I may not know what your dream is, but I know this: it's going to make a difference. Every God-sized dream does. Your dream might feel small. It might feel bigger than a mountain. But as we talked about in the very beginning, it's not the size of the dream that counts but instead the Giver of it.

Your dream may change the world in ways that make the front page of the news. Or it might change the world in ways that only your family knows. That doesn't reflect the importance of it but rather the purpose of it.

And I can guarantee this: you will not see the full impact of your dream this side of heaven. That can be one of the hardest parts.

All day long I click, type, look through the screen at the faces of people I love who live halfway across the country or even on the other side of the world. And sometimes, in the quiet moments, I wonder if what I do really makes a difference. "You can't see it in person," hisses the enemy. "You can't touch it. How do you know it's real?"

Then I think about how I should be doing something tangible—rocking a baby, handing out food, building a house. I feel a heart hunger to know the results with my five senses. I whisper this to Jesus one morning as sunlight spills in through the open window. I ask him if I've gotten it all wrong—if I should be doing something else. A verse pops into my heart like a present left on the front porch:

> Now faith is confidence in what we hope for and assurance about what we do not see. (Heb. 11:1)

I've always thought of those words in the context of believing in God. But that morning it seemed the One who loves us whispered that part of faith is also about believing that our obedience makes a difference—even when we can't see the results.

Sure of what we hope for . . . that what we do matters in the world, that hearts out there really are encouraged, that the flicker of our shining can bring light to a life again.

Certain of what we do not see . . . that the bonds we make, the needs we meet, the prayers we lift up are as real as what's right in front of us—that the great I Am is everywhere and in all we do in his name.

I think then of a conversation I had with my friend and fellow author Ann Voskamp many months ago about much the same thing. We tossed and turned thoughts around between us until at the end we nodded, smiled, and said . . .

How can we say that the virtual doesn't matter when the Spirit is virtual?

The kingdom has always been about more than what we can sense. Oh, friends, it's more about what we know in our hearts—and about following faithfully the One who whispers to us there—believing that in all things he is working together for good.

Sometimes that good is something we can see, touch, taste, and smell.

And sometimes it's built of eternal things that we won't know until heaven.

So press on, sisters.

Keep the faith.

Do what you do, be who you are, walk in that sometimes blind, always beautiful obedience.

Yes, you really are making a difference.

Your Dream Will Change You Too

When we begin a dream, it always seems to be about where we're going. We think of the future, the finish line, the results we want to see. Yet eventually we realize that this dream isn't about where we're going at all—it's really about who we're becoming along the way.

Yes, your dream will change the world. Even more, it will change you.

You are not the same person now that you were when you began to dream.

You will not be the same person you are today later on down the road.

The adventures we share with Jesus shape us from the inside out. We change, grow, stretch.

The other night I stayed up too late, curled under my covers with a book in hand. It spoke of things that made me take deep breaths and let them out slowly with relief. It spoke of freedom and grace and whispered that I am enough. In *The Me I Want to Be*, John Ortberg says:

> Here is the good news: When you flourish, you become more you. You become more that person God had in mind when God thought you up. You don't just become holier. You become you-ier. You will change: God wants you to become "a new creation." But "new" doesn't mean completely different; instead it's like an old piece of furniture that gets restored to its intended beauty. . . . God wants to redeem you, not exchange you.[16]

God-sized dreams are one of the main ways this happens in our lives. We think that God is concerned about us accomplishing a lot for him. But the God who spoke the world into being doesn't have any trouble with his to-do list. What he's interested in most is relationship. He wants to see you draw closer to him, become more like Jesus, and in doing so discover who you're truly meant to be as someone made in his image.

Becoming all you're created to be is simply saying yes to God whenever he asks you to grow with him.

You'll Be Glad You Did It

As I think back over the God-sized dreams in my life, both incredibly joyful and painful moments come to mind. But they all have one thing in common: I would do them again. Life is meant to be lived. Even what seems like the most colossal of mistakes in the moment can be redeemed by God.

It has been said that we all experience pain in our lives. As we've talked about, what we get to decide is whether it's the pain of risk or regret. There isn't a way to lead a completely safe life. And sometimes doing nothing is the greatest threat of all.

No one ever gets to their last breath and says, "I wish I hadn't said yes to Jesus so often. I could have had a much more comfortable life." As Jim Elliot, who lost his life for the gospel, said, "He is no fool who gives what he cannot keep to gain that what he cannot lose."[17] It's unlikely that you will have to literally die for your faith—but you will have to die to yourself. That's the paradox of a God-sized dream. It makes you come alive and causes you to die to yourself all at once.

You have a limitless, resurrected Jesus empowering you. He created you with strengths, gifts, and a calling that no one else will ever have. He has given you everything you need for a godly life (see 2 Pet. 1:3). He looks at you with love, has promised to be with you wherever you go, and will complete the good work he began in you.

Your God-sized dream is invincible with Jesus. Does that mean it will turn out the way you imagine? Nope. But it does mean that if you say yes to what God asks of you, he will complete his purposes in and through you. The greatest risk is not failure—it's disobedience.

You are not that kind of woman. I know it. You are already saying yes to what God asks just by reading these words, just by being open to dreaming. He will show you the next steps. He will make a way even when there seems to be none. He will guide you into all that he has for you.

And it will be amazing.

The "More" That Matters Most

We started our journey together talking about how we all long for more in our lives. Finding it seems like something mysterious. We wait for "more" to come to us. But here's the reality: most of the time we discover it along the way as we're saying yes to God.

The "more" we long for isn't something we can produce—instead it's something we receive. It's not found inside our comfort zones but instead just beyond them in the wild and glorious adventures God invites us to take with him.

You won't find "more" on your couch.

You won't find it in long hours at the office.

You won't find it in the new car parked in the driveway.

You won't even find it in your friends and family.

You'll only find it in the arms of Jesus.

Behind every "more" we dream of, he is what our hearts really want most. And they will never be satisfied with settling for anything less.

Consider the God-sized dreams in your heart as invitations to a fuller life. A life with more joy, passion, and growth. A life that makes you rejoice on the good days and push through the hard days because you know it's worth it.

You only get one shot at this world. And we only get one you. Make the most of your time here. Dare to dream. Dare to do. Dare to find out just how much God has in store for you.

I've loved sharing this journey with you. I wish we could end with a real-life conversation. I'd ask you all about what your heart has heard and your God-sized dream. I'd lean in and let you tell me all about it. I'd smile, nod, and cheer you on through every word. Before we left, I would pray for you too.

And until we get to have that face-to-face chat here or in heaven, I'm going to pray for you anyway . . . starting right now, right here as I type these words.

Lord,

Thank you for the one who is on this page right now. You know her name, her needs, her dreams. I thank you that she is a woman of faith and courage—a Joshua or Caleb in her generation. I thank you that even though she may feel some fear, she is saying yes to what you have placed in her heart to do.

As she finishes this book and goes about her day, I pray that you would continue the work you've started here. Guide her into the next step of her journey with you. Show her more of what you have in store for her. Provide what she needs all along the way.

I'm so glad you're with her the way I wish I could be today. Give her heart a hug for me. Help her with her dream. Thank you that it's going to change the world, her life, and eternity too.

Amen.

As we walked out the door of that little café, I'd say the four words we use in the South when we're feeling happy and want to encourage someone. Yes, here's a little send-off just for you . . .

"Go get 'em, friend!"

Go Deeper Guide

(Download a printable version with lines for writing at www.holley gerth.com on the "Books & More" page.)

1. *You are chosen.* What does God want you to do with your life—today, this week, in the future?
2. *You are already on your way.* What's one thing you can do right here, right now to make a difference and move a little closer to your God-sized dream?
3. *You're needed.* "The body is a unit, though it is made up of many parts; and though all its parts are many, they form one body" (1 Cor. 12:12 NIV 1984). What part of the body of Christ do you think you might be—heart, hands, eyes?
4. *You're loved.* What helps you hold on to God's love?
5. *You're going to make it.* What challenges are you facing right now? How will you get past them?
6. *Your dream is going to change the world.* At the end of your life, what do you want your legacy to be?
7. *Your dream will change you too.* How do you want to be different than you are right now a year from now, a decade from now, even longer? Growth is a lifelong process, and you will never stop until you're home.

Dream It. Do It.

It's time for you to close this book, my friend. And that means the most important thing you can do is to simply go out there and take the next step in your dream. What will it be? I'd like to know, and you can share it with me at www.holleygerth.com. You can also take a look at the e-coaching section of the site for one way I can partner with you in your God-sized dream.

Acknowledgments

The more I write, the more I realize it's about so much more than words on a page. It's really about a beautiful community of people joining together to birth something into the world.

Mark, thank you for helping me become the woman God created me to be and supporting my God-sized dreams. We make a great team, and I love you more every year.

My family (especially Mom, Dad, Stephen, Amber, Granny Eula, and Poppi) for showing me that words are a way of loving that can truly make a difference. You have prayed for all my dreams and cheered me on every step of the way. I'm so grateful.

Chip MacGregor, thanks for your work as my agent on this book. You're also a wise friend, a valued advisor, and one of the first who caught the vision.

Jennifer Leep, every time I think of how God gave you to me as my editor at Revell, I still get happy tears in my eyes. Your insight, friendship, and support have meant more to me than I can even express. I'm so glad we get to do this together again.

Twila Bennett, you are the queen of marketing, and I'm so thrilled to have found a fabulous friend as well as a wonderful partner on this project through you. We are like a pair of cute shoes at our favorite store (you know the one). The perfect match.

The DaySpring, Blessings Unlimited, and (in)courage teams—I am so blessed to do ministry and business with you.

The women of (in)courage—you are my extended network of sisters. If I listed all the ways each of you has blessed me, I would need to write another book! Thank you for your love, your grace, and the way you make me brave enough to go out there into the world with my words.

To my real-life girlfriends, thank you for all of the hours you spent talking with me about these things over coffee—for being my sounding board and safe place. You are a gift to me, and I thank God for you so often.

To my blog readers, thank you for sharing this journey with me. This book started with you, and you helped me grow this seed of an idea into what it is today. Your beautiful fingerprints are all over the place here.

To all the other God-sized dreamers in my life, thank you for what you've taught me about living with courage, taking leaps of faith, and being committed to growth and relationships for a lifetime.

Most of all, thank you to Jesus for being willing to use me just as I am. Let's keep dreaming together. I'm yours forever.

Notes

1. Rick Warren, *The Purpose Driven Life: What on Earth Am I Here For?* (Grand Rapids: Zondervan, 2003), 11.
2. You can read about the study at http://www.gammawomen.com.
3. "Citizenship in a Republic," speech at the Sorbonne, Paris, April 23, 1910, quoted at "In His Own Words," Theodore Roosevelt Association, http://www.theodoreroosevelt.org/life/quotes.htm.
4. Marcus Buckingham and Donald O. Clifton, *Now, Discover Your Strengths* (New York: Free Press, 2001).
5. Gretchen Rubin, *The Happiness Project: Or, Why I Spent a Year Trying to Sing in the Morning, Clean My Closets, Fight Right, Read Aristotle, and Generally Have More Fun* (New York: HarperCollins, 2009), 66–67.
6. Sharon Wooten, "I Really Need to Get Over It," (in)courage, July 21, 2001, http://www.incourage.me/2011/07/i-really-need-to-get-over-it.html.
7. Bruce Wilkinson, *The Dream Giver: Following Your God-Given Destiny* (Colorado Springs: Multnomah, 2003), 98.
8. Bonnie Gray, "A Tribute: Sara's Song & Why It's Hard to Say Goodbye," *Faith Barista* (blog), September 18, 2011, http://www.faithbarista.com/2011/09/a-tribute-sara-frankls-song-and-why-its-hard-to-say-goodbye/.
9. Laurel Mellin, *Wired for Joy* (Carlsbad, CA: Hay House, 2010), 2.
10. Timothy Ferriss, *The 4-Hour Workweek: Escape 9–5, Live Anywhere, and Join the New Rich*, expanded and updated ed. (New York: Crown, 2009), Kindle ed., 36–37.
11. Janet Kornblum, "Study: 25% of Americans Have No One to Confide In," *USA Today*, June 22, 2006, www.usatoday.com/news/nation/2006-06-22-friendship_x.htm.
12. Wilkinson, *The Dream Giver*, 110.
13. John Piper, *Don't Waste Your Life* (Wheaton: Crossway, 2003), 97.
14. Kristen Strong, "What Every Bit of Bad News Holds," *Chasing Blue Skies* (blog), November 29, 2011, http://chasingblueskies.net/?p=2685.

15. Jill Churchill, quoted in "Mother's Day Love and Appreciation," *Positive Impact*, May 8, 2012, http://www.positiveimpactmagazine.com/2011/05/06/mothers-day-love-and-appreciation/.
16. John Ortberg, *The Me I Want to Be: Becoming God's Best Version of You* (Grand Rapids: Zondervan, 2009), 16.
17. Jim Elliot, journal entry, October 28, 1949; archived at the Billy Graham Center, Wheaton, IL, http://www2.wheaton.edu/bgc/archives/faq/20.htm.

About Holley

Holley Gerth is a bestselling writer, life coach, and speaker who loves sharing God's heart with women through words. She's done so through several books, a partnership with DaySpring, and her popular blog. Holley is also a co-founder of (in)courage, a website for women that received almost a million page views in its first six months. Holley now does e-coaching for God-sized dreamers, and you can find out more about how she can partner with you at www.holleygerth.com.

Holley shares her heart and home with her husband, Mark. She lives in the South, likes to say "y'all," and would love to have coffee with you so she could hear all about you too. Until then, she hopes you'll hang out with her online at www.holleygerth.com.

Hello, friend!

Thanks again for sharing this journey with me. I truly wish I could have a cup of coffee with you today and hear about your God-sized dreams. Until then, I hope we can stay connected in some other ways!

I'd love for you to stop by and visit my place online at **www.holleygerth.com**. The e-coaching section will tell you about one way I can partner with you in your God-sized dream. And when you subscribe to my blog by email, you'll get free encouraging messages sent right to your inbox.

With Jesus you really are made for more, my friend. Keep believing that's true and dreaming like you do!

Love,

Holley Gerth

PS: Together we can help women all over the world fulfill their God-sized dreams. A portion of author proceeds from this book will go to the Compassion International Leadership Development Program. To find out more about the program, visit **www.compassion.com.**